# The Hybrid Cloud Handbook for AWS

AWS Cloud Networking for Traditional Network Engineers

Tim McConnaughy

# The Hybrid Cloud Handbook for AWS

AWS Cloud Networking for Traditional Network Engineers

Tim McConnaughy

ISBN 979-8-9878647-0-8

# Contents

# Copyright

# Foreword

**Stuart Clark – Senior Developer Advocate, Cisco Press Author, and DevNet Expert**

Cloud technology is quickly becoming the backbone of today's businesses and organizations, and network engineers need to be able to understand and manage the cloud infrastructure to ensure that their networks are secure, reliable, and efficient. Cloud-based services have allowed organizations to quickly adjust operations, scale up or down as needed, and provide remote access to critical applications and data. For example, cloud computing has enabled companies to quickly transition to remote work and videoconferencing, some of things were more challenging using traditional networks and infrastructure.

The network engineer of today, no longer just manages routers, switches, firewalls, and load-balancers. Network engineers are now creating and building their own tools. Previously this was challenging, as network engineer were bound to their employers and the infrastructure required to be productive just were not affordable on an individual basis or a POC (Proof of Concept). Network teams wishing to build even something as trivial as a monitoring platform or distributed infrastructure resource modelling (IRM) application quickly got confronted by an unfortunate reality: most of the necessary building blocks were available only under commercial licenses or they were locked out as this was not the network. To get anything done, they needed someone to approve budget, which often resulted in weeks of building presentations and rationalization. Cloud technology also makes it easier for network engineers to quickly implement new services and applications, allowing them to be more agile and responsive to the needs of their company, partners, or customers.

So, the cloud eats us all for breakfast? No. Cloud technology is designed to complement, rather than replace, existing IT infrastructure and systems. Network engineers needed to design, develop, deploy, and manage cloud solutions, as well as to monitor and maintain the underlying networks and systems. In addition, cloud technology is constantly evolving, and network engineers will need to stay on top of the latest developments to ensure that cloud-based solutions are secure, reliable, and up to date. Most networks are now Hybrid, this helps to improve ROI (Return of Investment) by providing organizations with the flexibility to use a combination of public and private cloud services to meet their needs. This enables organizations to optimize their cloud usage and costs, as well as to maximize their use of existing on-premises infrastructure. Hybrid cloud also allows organizations to quickly deploy new services and applications, making them more agile and responsive to customer needs. Additionally, hybrid cloud enables organizations to better manage their data and workloads, allowing them to achieve greater efficiencies and cost savings.

Sign me up, how do I start? There is a plethora of information, books, course out there. So why not learn from someone who has done this themselves. What the author has written here is your step into the cloud and hybrid world, and a guide to get you started on your career for the next five years.

Tim has a deep understanding of cloud technologies and networks and has formulated a blueprint and helps the reader get familiar with cloud computing basics, starting off by learning the basics of cloud computing, types of cloud services, terminology, and the advantages and disadvantages of cloud computing. He has taken the time explain complex concepts in simple and understandable language for level of experiences. He clearly articulates the key points of the cloud technologies and provide examples to illustrate his point. You will find all chapters consistent and in an organized manner, which ensures a smooth and enjoyable reading and learning experience.

Today, network engineers are unquestionably one of the most important assets a business has, regardless of what industry it is in. Thus, this new era offers an exciting and unprecedented opportunity: to take pride in this status and ownership of these new responsibilities and technologies.

**Du'An Lightfoot, Sr. Cloud Networking Developer Advocate.**

In 2013 my organization decided to implement lean manufacturing to save costs. This required the development of a new application. To support this project, my task was to build out a new network infrastructure. The switches, servers, and storage alone expensed for well over $300,000. The planning and purchasing of this hardware took about 6 months. And that's not including the time to build and deploy the hardware.

Imagine repeating this process for every new network or application an organization needs. At that pace an organization maybe able to release 1 new application a year. And we have not mentioned the need to scale the infrastructure up or out. If there is a larger than expected demand for your application you will need to buy more servers, memory, switches, firewalls, routers and then repeat the entire procurement process again. There's no way a company can compete like that in 2023.

This problem has led companies to change how they develop and deliver their applications and services. By leveraging a cloud first principal companies are able to build, deploy, and scale infrastructure and applications in minutes. And the cost savings of using the cloud is inherent. Because you are only charged for the services you use in the cloud. Rather than on-prem. Where you have the upfront costs of servers, ram and storage resources that you may never use.

But there's still another problem. With this new shift there are new skills that network engineers need to obtain. As a network engineer my first experience with the cloud was with connecting VPNs to AWS. But because my role was siloed, I could only focus on the on-premises side of this connectivity. Many network engineers I know have faced the same scenario.

In this book Tim has done a great job of peeling back the curtain of the cloud. He speaks in the language that network engineers can understand. He takes the skills of a traditional network engineer and relates them to cloud networking constructs. Which will help to equip you with an understanding of the fundamental building blocks of cloud networking on AWS. Remember, technology is always evolving and as a network engineer we have to always evolve with it. Use this book as a guide to help you on your evolution. Keep going and embrace the tech journey!

# Getting Started

## Who Should Read This Book?

This book is intended for the everyday network engineer. Whatever your vendor of choice, be it Cisco, Juniper, Arista, or some Whitebox solution, this book is intended for the network warriors that keep the infrastructure running and the packets moving.

## Why This Book?

Every one of us are the firefighters, the first responders (or second, or third...) to the needs of our respective organizations and businesses, and that doesn't leave a ton of time for much else. All of us are at different points in our careers: starting out, juniors, seniors, architects, and senior architects. The common theme is that though our actual responsibilities are different, what we all lack equally is time. Time to learn the next big thing. Time to learn the current big thing. Most of us lack time to get the work done that's sitting on our plate, much less spend extra time to add three more things. So, what do network engineers without time to eat what's on their own plate do when told to eat off another plate too?

That's why this book exists. We aren't here to learn everything there is to know about cloud computing. We aren't here to learn everything there is to know about cloud networking, even. But whether we like it or not, the future is hybrid cloud, or hybrid data center, if you prefer. The lines between the 'cloud team', which focuses mostly on apps, and the 'network team', which has heretofore only managed on-prem, is blurring. So, let's focus on the vocabulary, and how it relates back to what we already know. Let's be laser focused and frugal with our time so we can keep up and still catch up.

## Who Shouldn't Read This Book?

If you are a cloud engineer, a data scientist, an app developer, or someone looking to get a certification in cloud computing, this book may not be the right one for you. The goal of this book is to serve as a Rosetta Stone for traditional network engineers to understand and interact with cloud networking. While we absolutely will discuss topics that are relevant to all the above roles and reasons, we'll be doing it from a network engineering perspective. Without the background in network engineering, the value of this book will be diminished.

# The Basics of Cloud Networking

Before we get started in earnest, we should take a moment to set expectations. You, dear reader, are unlikely to emerge from the other side of this book as a beautiful cloud butterfly, a shining star and paragon of cloud ethos, pathos, and logos. Sorry. It's important to get that out right up front.

Actually becoming an expert in cloud networking will take time and effort. There is no hack or shortcut to the end. What you should come out of this book with is the ability to have meaningful conversations with the cloud teams about how to build a robust hybrid cloud/data center network, using terminology and network concepts everyone understands.

Now, without further ado, let's get started.

## The Cloud is a Fabric

This is probably the least surprising thing you'll learn in this book. Perhaps the second least surprising, right after, "The cloud is just someone else's data center". That gets repeated everywhere, let's assume that's the real least surprising thing. Every Cloud Service Provider (CSP from now on) has some version of a fabric topology driving all the networking and compute under the covers. Do you have to be an expert on fabric technologies to understand cloud networking? No, absolutely not. If that seems odd, ask yourself, "Do I have to be an expert at MPLS technologies to peer with a service provider?"

We're establishing the fact that the cloud is a fabric to help set the stage for some of the reasons behind how cloud networking functions. If you don't want to know or don't care about how it all works under the covers (and no one would blame you, we all have plenty to learn without needing to memorize things we have no control over), we can stop at a simple description of how fabrics generally operate. For those that want to learn how deep the rabbit hole goes, Toni Pasanen's excellent books, "AWS Networking Fundamentals" and "Azure Networking Fundamentals" offer a much deeper dive into the fabrics powering the cloud. There will be links to them in the appendix.

Broadly speaking, a cloud fabric is an arbitrary network topology based on creating tunnels over an underlying physical topology. This fabric may consist of any or all tunneling technologies such as IPsec, GRE, VXLAN, etc. Facilitating the tunneling is a vast underlay of SDN-orchestrated switches and routers, similar to Cisco ACI or Arista Converged Cloud Fabric. Basic connectivity is established between an ocean of network devices, and on top of that is orchestrated this arbitrary fabric that serves as the customer-facing 'cloud network'.

Each customer is separated into their isolated environment, and within this tenancy, the customer is free to create their own self-directed network within the confines of what the CSP allows. It is at this level that we, the network engineers, enter the picture.

Because of this, cloud network engineering (at least the part we can engineer) starts with Layer 3 of the OSI model. This is great for those of us who've been designing networks for 20 years to overcome the limitations imposed by Layer 2. No broadcast storms, no spanning tree, and no goofy MAC learning issues with switching (that we can cause, or fix). Here's a sneak peek at what we'll be covering.

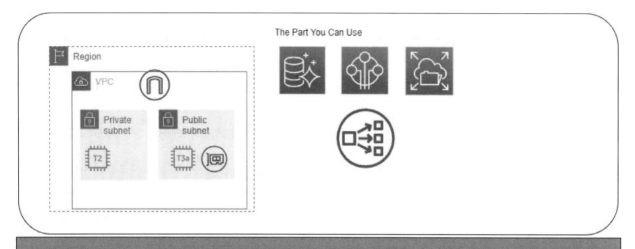

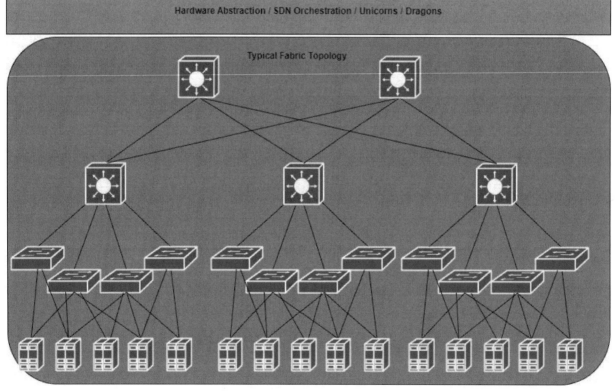

Figure 1: Typical Cloud Fabric

# The CSP is an MSP

The main thing to remember about the CSPs is that they operate just like the MSPs, or managed service providers, that network engineers are already familiar with. They have service offerings, they manage the infrastructure, and you can change only what they allow you to change. In the case of the cloud, it's all done via a self-service web portal (or API, or Infrastructure as Code), rather than the traditional MSP method of opening a ticket or calling a service desk. This is an important way to think about consuming the cloud, and especially about how to interact with it. The CSP is going to give you varying levels of control over the network constructs, usually the bare minimum required. Beyond the bare minimum connectivity offers, expect to pay an upcharge for just about any managed connectivity solutions, both for the solution itself and often data transfer charges as well.

Cloud networking can be extremely cost-effective with proper network design that minimizes charges, but it can also be extremely costly if designed poorly and without proper controls in place. This book does not aim to make a cloud financial expert out of anyone, but it should be noted that a large value proposition of the cloud cannot be realized without proper attention paid to how the data must move. Now, more than ever, we are on the front lines of making good architecture decisions to save money.

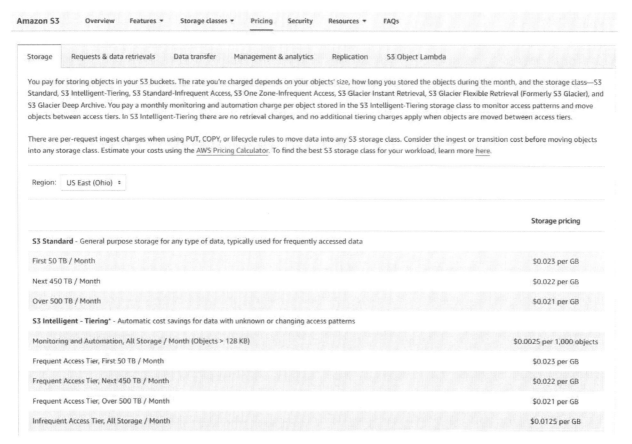

**Figure 2: Sample Data Transfer Charges**

The above sample table was taken from: https://docs.aws.amazon.com/solutions/latest/data-transfer-hub/cost.html and is representative of the consumption model of cloud costing.

# The Basics of AWS Networking

Now let us continue to dive into the cloud networking constructs and relate them back to the traditional network concepts with which we are familiar. Within each section, we will discuss the construct and its details before explaining in what more traditional terms it makes sense. Fair warning, some cloud constructs have no on-prem equivalent, and the best that can be done is to explain it in terms which combines things that don't usually work together. Wherever possible, examples, diagrams and terminology will be used to maximize understanding.

## VPC

We begin with the simplest and most important network construct within AWS: The humble VPC. VPC stands for Virtual Private Cloud, which makes it sound like the entire environment in which you might build your cloud network. It would be more accurate to refer to a VPC as a self-contained routed domain.

### Architecture

Here is an example of a standard VPC diagram that you might find on any AWS documentation:

**Figure 3: Typical Basic VPC Diagram**

This is a diagram of two different VPCs, split between AWS regions. We'll end up talking about regions plenty, but it's important to focus on the VPCs here for the moment. If the above diagram is tough to understand, how about this one?

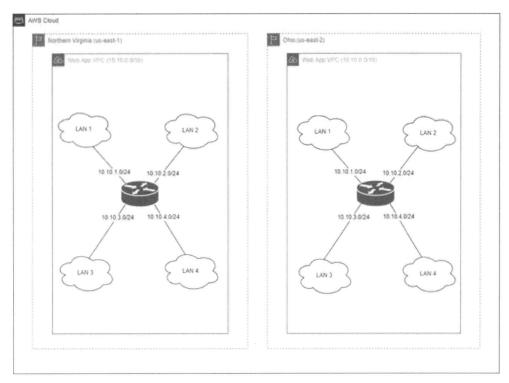

**Figure 4: VPC Network Architecture Simplified**

A VPC is really just a routed domain. Within each VPC is a hidden cloud construct which serves as the router for the VPC. If resources are created within the VPC, the VPC router ensures those resources have connectivity to each other with no route table manipulation or interface configuration required. Imagine having a single router connected to no other routers but connecting some manner of network segments directly to each interface, you would have the basic construct of a VPC. The VPC construct is irrevocably tied to the CIDR allocated to it when created. This supernet can be as large as a /16 or as small as a /28. Each VPC has a main CIDR block, created with the VPC itself, which can be further subdivided into subnets (more on that in a moment). Further, each VPC can have more CIDRs allocated after creation, so long as those CIDRs do not overlap each other, as seen below:

**AWS VPC Console - 2023**

Only the main VPC CIDR gets the 'automatic' services like DNS and DHCP, which we'll cover soon.

The other CIDRs are just extra IP space if needed. Importantly, IPv6 CIDRs cannot be built this way. They must be be allocated by AWS, added to AWS if you own your own block of IPs, or use AWS IP Address Management (IPAM). AWS pre-creates a Default VPC in each region. This VPC is created in every AWS region for your account and serves as a launchpad for using the cloud. The Default VPC uses 172.31.0.0/16 as the CIDR, and that is further subdivided into subnets based on how many Availability Zones a region has.

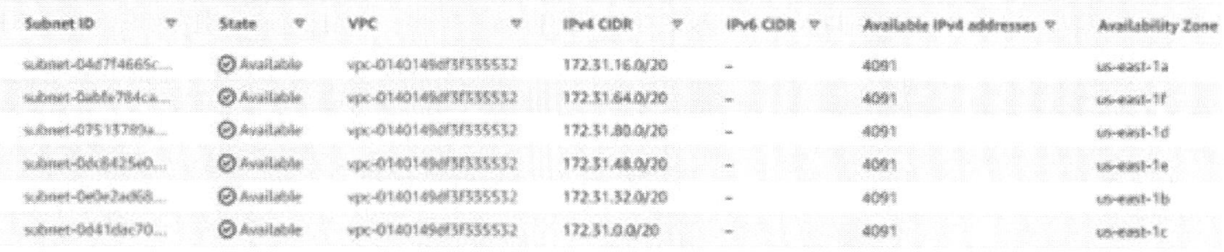

| Subnet ID | State | VPC | IPv4 CIDR | IPv6 CIDR | Available IPv4 addresses | Availability Zone |
|---|---|---|---|---|---|---|
| subnet-04d7f4665c... | Available | vpc-0140149df3f335532 | 172.31.16.0/20 | – | 4091 | us-east-1a |
| subnet-0ab6e784ca... | Available | vpc-0140149df3f335532 | 172.31.64.0/20 | – | 4091 | us-east-1f |
| subnet-07513789a... | Available | vpc-0140149df3f335532 | 172.31.80.0/20 | – | 4091 | us-east-1d |
| subnet-0dc8425e0... | Available | vpc-0140149df3f335532 | 172.31.48.0/20 | – | 4091 | us-east-1e |
| subnet-0e0e2ad68... | Available | vpc-0140149df3f335532 | 172.31.32.0/20 | – | 4091 | us-east-1b |
| subnet-0d41dac70... | Available | vpc-0140149df3f335532 | 172.31.0.0/20 | – | 4091 | us-east-1c |

Figure 5: Default VPC Subnet Deployment

This VPC doesn't have to be used for anything, and so you may be asking, "Why does AWS create one?" Remember two things about the origins of cloud: It was created for developers, not network engineers, and most AWS services (including and beyond EC2 Virtual Machine services) do require some sort of network to allow the services to communicate. The Default VPC was created to give developers a sandbox to allow development without having to understand networking, giving them an environment to create applications.

## Subnets and Availability Zones

Each VPC consists of a supernet (like 172.31.0.0/16) and each subnet within that VPC is subdivided into smaller slices. Let's discuss Availability Zones, Regions, and subnets in AWS, because they are all linked. Here's a basic diagram to explain what an AWS Region and Availability Zone are in real terms:

**Figure 6: Sample Region and Availability Zone Map**

An AWS Region is a geographical area of the world within which AWS has designated it will operate. It has no true borders or boundaries except the ones AWS has defined. In reality, the operating border of an AWS Region is probably closely tied to its Point of Presence attachment to the AWS global backbone, but AWS does not disclose these details.

Within each Region are several Availability Zones. These AZs are, loosely, some form of AWS data center. The physical location of each data center is not publicly available, but each AZ falls within the jurisdiction and border of an AWS Region. Each AWS account has their AZ list randomized when first created as a form of load balancing. This means that one account's AZ-A, B and C might be a different physical data center than another account's AZ-A, B and C. Ultimately, this helps AWS load balance consumption, but could complicate network planning if multiple accounts were to be involved with creating the network, potentially introducing undetectable fate sharing. The chances are extremely low, but not impossible, that two different accounts building network virtual appliances to peer might end up in the same physical data center (or physical rack, potentially) despite both picking different AZs to deploy in. For this reason (and others, such as billing), it's common for one network engineering account to own the network. For completeness, it should be noted that there is a way to enforce cross-account consistency using AZ IDs, which we'll cover more when we talk about AWS PrivateLink.

Not all AZs contain the exact same compute, storage, and network gear. This fact has caused constant frustration with engineers looking to plan their cloud deployments only to stumble when the planned AZ lacks a certain virtual machine type or managed service. AWS is always expanding their services and physical locations, however, meaning that over time the tendency is to reach feature parity across a region. As far as subnets, each subnet is tied to an AZ and a VPC. The VPC is tied to the Region, while subnets are tied to an AZ. Multiple subnets can inhabit the same AZ or different subnets can be spread across multiple AZs for redundancy, but a single subnet can only inhabit one AZ. Let's look at a common deployment for a VPC full of highly available servers:

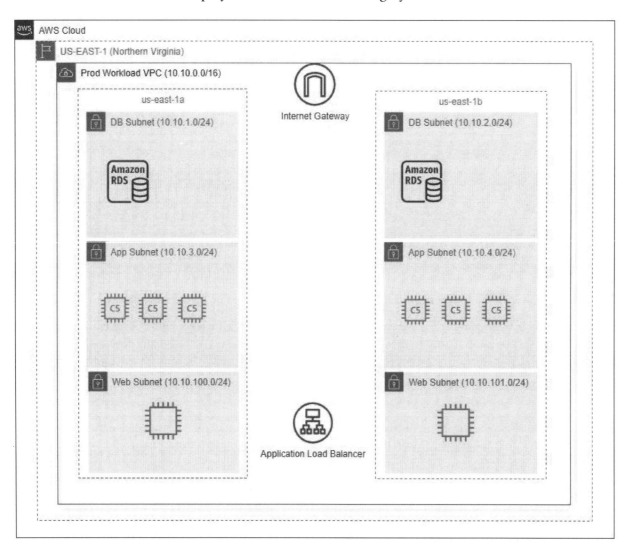

**Figure 7: Common 3 Tier Web App Cloud Deployment**

Seems easy right? Remember the invisible router sitting in the VPC, handling the connectivity across all these subnets as if each subnet were an attached interface and network segment.

Importantly, the applications themselves are usually deployed in a highly available configuration. In this design, servers in AZ-A will not send traffic to servers in AZ-B to lessen cross-AZ data transfer charges, instead each AZ will act as its own app stack servicing web requests from the Internet. If an AZ fails, a second app stack is still up and running.

Why does that matter to a network engineer? Because subnets work differently in the cloud than they do in an on-prem environment. You may have already thought of the questions, "If the cloud doesn't have broadcast domains, why use separate subnets at all? Why not throw every device into one or two subnets instead of creating all these other ones?"

Two reasons. One, as mentioned, a subnet is tied to an AZ, so if redundancy is needed, more subnets are needed. Two, subnets provide a boundary to which we can apply security. Again, think of a subnet as a network segment attached to a router interface. Where the router is involved, we can apply things like network access control lists (NACL). Understanding how the application tiers communicate is important so that we as network engineers can properly scope data flows and secure the environment.

We'll cover cloud security later in the book, for now, it's important to understand the need for subnets and how it differs from the needs of a traditional network.

## DHCP and DNS Services

In addition to being a simple routed domain, the humble VPC offers two other very important services to facilitate elasticity and ease of use: DHCP and DNS. DHCP works as you would expect, though in a cloud fabric of course there is no need to track the DHCP Discover, Offer, Request and Acknowledgement. Think of the VPC Router in this context as being configured as a DHCP and DNS server. Of course, each VPC can be configured to use an actual DHCP and DNS server, but by default the VPC handles the allocation of IP addresses and provides DNS registration and lookup. Remembering the origins of cloud, this fits with the developer-focused model. Developers didn't know and didn't care to manage these services, so the VPCs handle the basic connectivity and services natively.

AWS reserves several IP addresses in each subnet, and the minimum size of any subnet in AWS is a /28, or 16 total addresses. If the CIDR of a given subnet is 10.10.0.0/24 as an example, this is the IP allocation reserved by AWS:

| IP Address | Usage |
|------------|-------|
| 10.10.0.0 | Network Address |
| 10.10.0.1 | VPC Router IP (and usually default gateway) |
| 10.10.0.2 | DNS services for subnet |
| 10.10.0.3 | Reserved for future use |
| 10.10.0.255 | Broadcast address, though broadcast is not supported, the address is still reserved |

Table 1: Reserved IP Addresses in a Subnet

AWS does support a more robust DHCP/DNS offering, of course. Here is an example of a custom DHCP option set that can be applied to a VPC.

Figure 8: Custom DHCP Option Set for VPC

There are a couple other details about how DHCP works and how addresses can be used which may have already been something you were wondering about. Yes, we can set aside addresses within a subnet to be explicitly assigned, taking them out of the DHCP scope that AWS uses to auto-assign IP addresses to resources. This can be done by a prefix or an explicit host reservation.

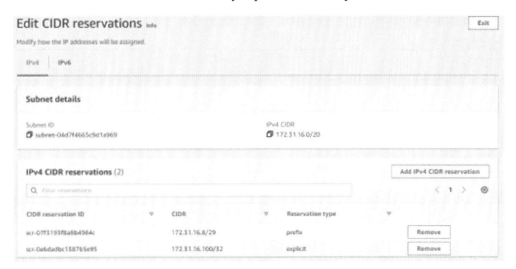

Moving on, DNS settings default to AWS Route 53, the cloud-native DNS server that will handle the internal and external DNS zone lookups for the VPC. If another DNS server is preferred, the DNS server IPs can be delivered via DHCP option set to VMs created in the VPC.

Without adding an entire chapter to this book on DNS, what is important is that by default, resources created in the VPC will be assigned a private IP and private DNS hostname/record automatically by AWS. This allows the resource to be accessible by name internally and externally across AWS, so long as connectivity exists. Route 53 also acts as the VPC DNS resolver for internal and external lookups, which historically makes life a lot easier for developers that don't know how to manage DNS services.

The DNS resolution and assignment services can be turned off if not needed. Some customers use a dedicated AWS DNS service, some use only on-prem DNS, and some do both. The full capabilities are way beyond the scope of this book, but as network engineers it's important to know what options exist. There's an excellent deeper dive available to understand all the different combination of VPC DNS settings here: https://docs.aws.amazon.com/vpc/latest/userguide/vpc-dns.html#vpc-dns-support

# VPC Routing

It's time to start digging into the real meat of cloud networking. We've already discussed the concept of a VPC router, but it's important to build a strong understanding of what to expect (and not expect) from it. Routing in the cloud isn't so different from the way we do it in traditional networks, but our level of visibility and control is.

## The VPC Router Redux

Some of us might remember the Cisco small business routers, the RV series. They might even still be around in some capacity. These routers default to web interface GUIs to configure and administrate.

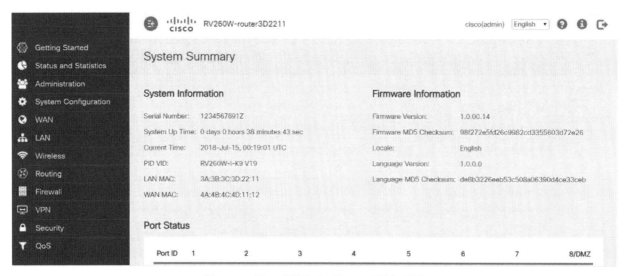

**Figure 9: Cisco RV Series Router Web GUI**

This screenshot was taken from: https://www.cisco.com/c/en/us/support/docs/smb/routers/cisco-rv-series-small-business-routers/smb381-accessing-the-web-based-setup-page-of-cisco-vpn-routers.html

For most of us, the idea of trying to do serious configuration of a router via a web GUI is anathema. The frustration of having to click through multiple menus just to turn up an interface or apply an IP address is only exceeded by the frustration of not being able to apply a particular configuration because the web GUI doesn't have a button for it. Welcome to the VPC Router! The VPC Router is a logical construct in AWS, as discussed before, but it does serve some of the essential functions expected of routers. It can route between subnets, it can apply security policy at the network level, and it acts as a default gateway for resources within a VPC. Rather than configuring the VPC router with a traditional CLI, the router can be configured indirectly by manipulating other constructs.

For example:

• Subnets

• Route Tables

• Network ACLs

• DHCP Option Sets

• Internet / NAT Gateways

Some of these we've talked briefly about, and others will be covered in later sections.

Understand that native cloud networking is very heavy on static routing, and there are very few constructs which do dynamic routing at all. Of those, expect to leave all the IGP routing protocols behind. The cloud runs on BGP, and not all BGP features are supported.

## The Route Table

The clearest indicator that the VPC router exists (despite being invisible and only indirectly configurable) is the Route Table. Here's a diagram that shows how the default route table of a VPC works:

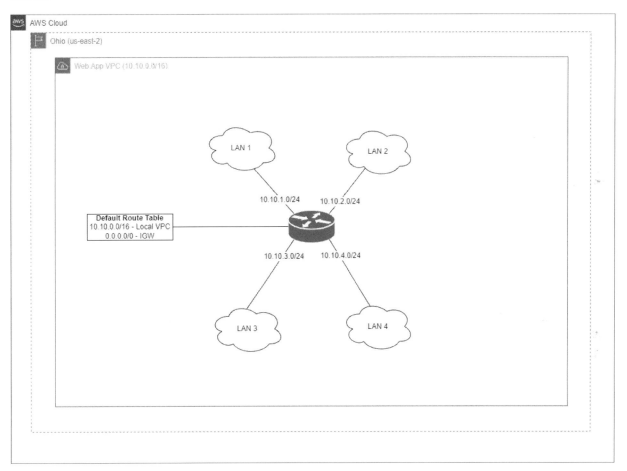

**Figure 10: Standard VPC Route Table**

This might seem a little underwhelming. It's all right, take all the time you need to come to terms with your disappointment.

The default VPC comes with an Internet Gateway (IGW) attached, a basic Route Table and not much else. If you create a custom VPC, AWS does not even assume you want an IGW and so only the Main Route Table is included, with that single entry. Local supernet routes are routed locally.

Remember that we likened the VPC to a single routed domain. In that context, this route table should make sense. The VPC router handles all routing between hosts, services and subnets created within the VPC. Every destination is local and there are no actual separate interfaces, so there is no need to maintain a complex route table.

We are glossing over the IGW because we will explore that in the section on Internet connectivity. Don't worry, all things in time. As far as 'local' routing, the resources inside a VPC are of course no more physically 'local' than they would be in a complex data center fabric spanning multiple racks. The concept of local VPC routing is logical. Each VPC comes with a main route table, created with the VPC.

This is akin to the global routing table on a router and governs the routing within the VPC for subnets that don't have other route tables attached.

This is a critical piece of new information, so it bears repeating. Each subnet within a VPC can be used with a custom route table if required, but the subnet can only have one route table at a time. This is like setting a VRF on a router interface attached to a network segment. Consider the following diagram:

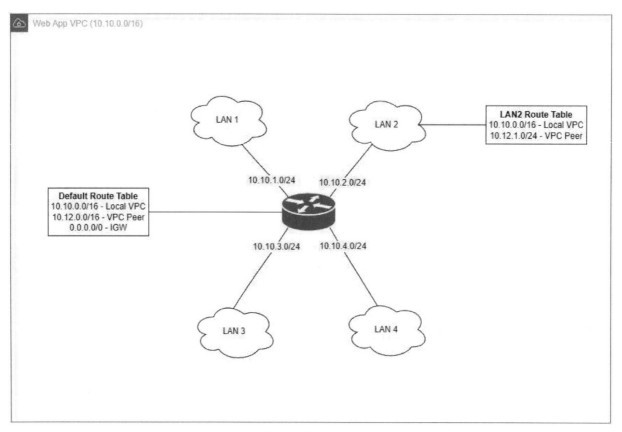

**Figure 11: Subnet with Custom Route Table**

Why would anyone do this, and how does it work? Imagine if LAN 2 contained sensitive workloads that should not have access to the Internet, but the VPC has an IGW attached for other servers that need to pull data from an Internet source. With custom Route Table attachment, the resources in each subnet can follow their own specific routing rules as if they are isolated to their own VRF.

It's not exactly like a VRF, because the resources in LAN 2 would still be able to communicate with any of the other LANs in this example. Speaking in terms of a local VPC, It's more like selective route filtering. This is another powerful benefit afforded by subdividing a VPC into subnets: they allow us to affect route policy more granularly.

Explaining each custom route table as a VRF helps visualize the behavior better but remember that it's not true network segmentation. The VPC router is like a fusion router in that respect, allowing each segment to communicate as long as the segment is local. Later, when we expand to include communication between VPCs and other services the idea of route-table-as-VRF will be more important.

It's important to reinforce that AWS has a concept of 'private' and 'public' subnets. The subnets themselves are classified as private or public based on the presence or absence of a default route to the Internet. So for Figure 11, LAN2 would be considered a private subnet, while the other subnets using the main route table would be considered a public subnet due to the default route to the IGW.

## Routing Between Subnets

Using what we've learned so far, let's think a little about the possibilities that a custom Route Table in a VPC could be used for when routing traffic between subnets. Remember, the actual data path will not be transiting a router as it would with a physical deployment, but we can affect data plane traffic as if it were in some cases. Let's imagine a VPC with strict, if somewhat odd, requirements for LAN2 subnet traffic. Here are the requirements:

• LAN2 subnet must only communicate with LAN4 subnet.

• LAN2 subnet must not have access to the Internet.

It's not yet time to dive into Network ACLs, so we need to focus on the routing options to accomplish the requirement. How would we implement this behavior by using Route Tables? Surely it should be a matter of removing the other subnets from the LAN2 custom route table?

Well, not exactly. There is a sticky route in every Route Table that can't be moved or removed, and that is the VPC CIDR route for the local VPC. We can add and remove more specific routes within the local VPC, and we can do the same with destinations outside the local VPC, but the VPC CIDR supernet route will always be there to ensure connectivity within the VPC. We can change the target or next-hop of this VPC CIDR route, however.

**Editing Route Table Entries**

Honestly, however, the reasons for doing this are slim. In almost all real-world cases, what you would do instead is leave the supernet route alone and insert more specific routes to move traffic between source and destination in a more granular, deterministic way.

What if instead of using the VPC router for routing, we wanted to use a network virtual appliance? The VPC router would still be the default gateway for resources, but the VPC router would redirect traffic to the specified target based on longest-prefix matching, just like a traditional router.

We'll be talking a lot more about NVA (network virtual appliance) usage later, but to pull back the curtain a bit, what if the goal was to have traffic between two subnets be inspected by a virtual firewall appliance? What if instead of the requirements from earlier, the new requirements instead were:

• LAN2 to LAN4 traffic (and vice versa) must be inspected by a firewall.

• LAN2 and LAN4 subnet must not have access to the Internet.

How would the VPC router and Route Tables help make this happen?

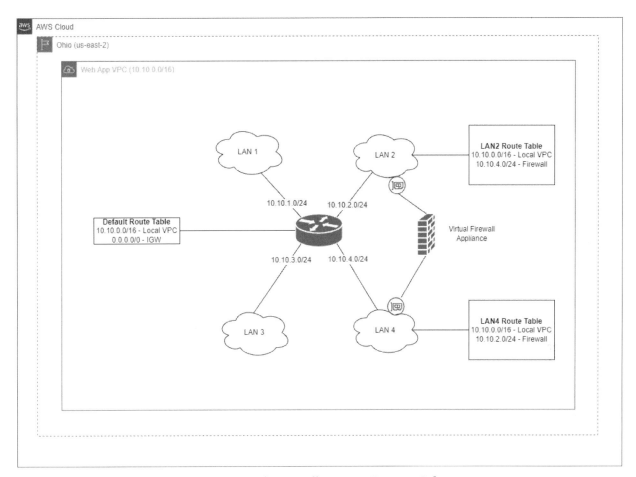

**Figure 12: Sample Firewall Insertion Between Subnets**

The curtain is being pulled back a little more than you might be ready for, so let's break it down.

Remember that each subnet can have a custom Route Table, or it can use the VPC main route table. For LAN1 and LAN3, that's exactly what is happening because there are no special requirements.

LAN2 and LAN4 have the same (mirrored) requirement, but we know that from a routing perspective the sources and destinations are different. That means using different custom Route Tables. We've left the VPC local route entry in the route table alone but inserted a new route for a specific destination because we want the data path to be different for traffic between those two subnets.

For the purposes of exposition, let's assume we spun up your favorite firewall in the VPC with two network interfaces (in addition to the management interface), and placed an interface in the two LAN subnets denoted by the NIC icon. We can then make the firewall interface itself be the target of a route rather than needing to specify a specific IP address. This is a wild disjoint from how we consider traditional networking. The firewall NIC has an IP address associated with it, likely assigned via DHCP in the subnet. The Route Table doesn't use the IP of the NIC as the next hop, however. Looking at the "Edit Route Table Entries" picture above, we can see that entering an IP address as the destination is not supported.

This is something of a mind blower to traditional network engineers but recall that the cloud fabric is tracking every host, object, and service, including the network interfaces. There's a whole section about Elastic Network Interfaces coming up after this, but it was necessary to give a sneak peek now to explain some of the ways we can route traffic between VPC subnets (and later, outside of VPCs entirely). For now, focus on the fact that the VPC Route Tables allow us to specify different paths for different traffic, just like a real router. Longest prefix still determines the best path, and the destinations are object-based, not IP-based.

Keep this is mind as we move forward to talk about a concept that is usually wholly new to traditional network engineers: the Elastic Network Interface.

# Elastic Network Interface

The ENI is a tough concept to wrap your head around for many network engineers, but it shouldn't be. The cloud fabric is managed and orchestrated by a large, automated SDN. It stands to reason that everything with an IP address is tracked and managed by that same SDN. For those familiar with VXLAN or LISP fabrics, host location tracking is well known. ENI is essentially a host entry in the fabric that can be assigned or reassigned to various virtual machines and services within the cloud. An ENI is either created automatically when a virtual machine is created via an AWS Amazon Machine Image (like an OVA/OVF in VMWare, it's a blueprint of virtual hardware for a VM), or, in the case of certain network-aware services, it can be created when activating the service or added later if needed. The ENI serves to provide network connectivity and is tied to a particular VPC and subnet where that VM or service needs the connectivity. An ENI is tied to the Availability Zone in which it is created. Usually the ENI will be allocated a private IP when created that follows the ENI until moved to another subnet or deleted.

In the case of virtual machines that network engineers should already be familiar with (firewalls, routers, load balancers) an ENI is just an extension of the virtual machine. The ENI can be attached at creation, as mentioned before, or an ENI can be created on its own and then attached to a VM or service. Not every VM can handle this hot swapping well, and they may need to be restarted to pick up the addition or subtraction of the ENI. In 90% of cases, the ENI functions exactly like a VNIC in VMWare or another virtualized network card. The biggest difference is that the ENI can be attached, detached, exist entirely on its own, and be moved between the VMs and services within an Availability Zone.

Here is an example of an ENI swap that should help this concept make sense using the scenario we used earlier:

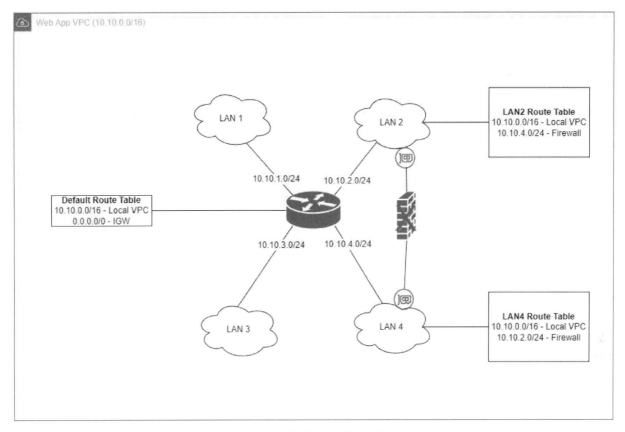

**Figure 13: Failed Firewall Appliance**

With health checking and automation, we could recover from failures quickly in the cloud. Let's suppose that we have some sort of health checking on the firewall because it is in a critical application data path. We also have automation that can act based on failure detection. Now suppose the virtual firewall appliance fails. Perhaps the rack of compute it was running in has failed, or just the virtualization host. The automation is set up to instantiate a new running firewall and move the ENIs to that new appliance.

Why do we need to do that?

Remember that the static routes for the subnets have been set up to route traffic between LAN2 and LAN4 through those specific ENIs. We could go fix the Route Tables to point at the new firewall's ENIs, but wouldn't it be easier to just move those ENIs to the new appliance instead?

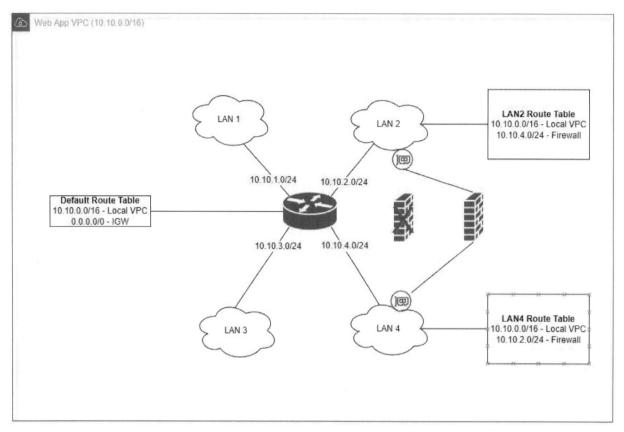

**Figure 14: Example ENI Swap for Failure**

By detaching the ENI from the old, failed appliance and attaching it to the new one, we could recover from failure very quickly (and automatically). With automation all things are possible. We could also have used automation to update those Route Tables to point at brand new ENIs created with the new firewall. This example is focused on understanding the mobility of an ENI, though, so that was the path we chose.

Importantly, an ENI also has to be configured to forward traffic instead of just accepting it. By default, the ENI will drop traffic not destined for the VM itself. When using NVAs, then, it is common to disable the source/destination check so that the packets destined for other VMs will be accepted for forwarding.

Above all things, remember that an ENI is just a logical construct. Think of it as a reserved host entry in a fabric that can move and be reassigned to other hosts. This is an easier concept for engineers with prior understanding of how host tracking works in fabrics, but it's not that tough a concept. The SDN carries a host entry for a particular IP address and the fabric is aware of the networks and hosts it is currently assigned to, sending traffic there. Should an ENI be detached and reattached elsewhere, the SDN just updates the fabric with the new location information. This is a powerful way to leverage SDN for high availability.

# Connecting AWS Networks Together

Now that we have a decent understanding of the features and limitations of cloud networking, let's expand our horizons to connect AWS cloud networks together. This is still a mostly static affair, which means as our network grows, the time cost of administrating it will grow as well. Here are some ways we can connect AWS VPCs and services together.

## Native VPC Peering

The simplest and easiest option to connect two VPCs together is native VPC peering. This peering essentially sets up a fabric connection in the AWS underlay that allows traffic to be sent between two isolated networks privately. This point-to-point peering connection can be established between a single account or multiple accounts and can be within the same region or across regions as well. There is a request/accept workflow in establishing the VPC peer where both accounts (or the single account) involved must send a peer request, and the other side must accept that request.

The result of a successful peering request sets up the private peer connectivity. It should be noted that the peering is an object, and that object itself does nothing but represent the underlay connection. The Route Tables must still be configured to direct traffic to the peer connection.

Here is a diagram of a native peer VPC setup.

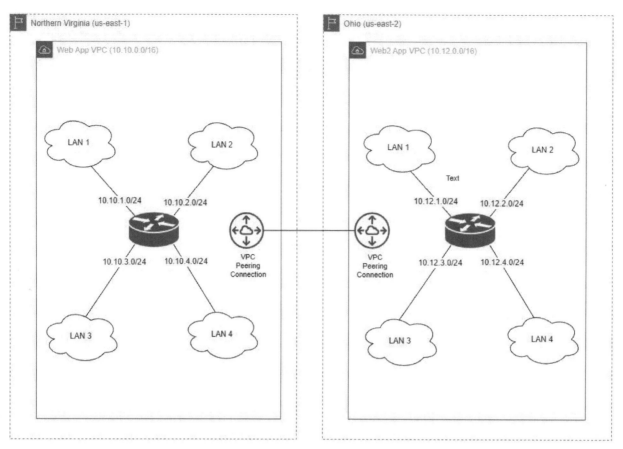

Figure 15: Inter-Region VPC Peering

This setup happens to be inter-region, but the behavior is the same within a region. In each of these VPCs, a new object is available to be the target for Route Table updates. That object is the VPC peer attachment. When two VPCs are natively peered, there are some expectations to manage. Here's a concise list of what to expect and what not to expect:

• Route Tables in both VPCs can use the VPC peering attachment as a target for any routes, if the intention is to send that traffic to the other VPC. Any traffic sent across the VPC peer link needs to be destined to a target in the destination VPC, though the destination CIDR itself could be different. Clarification on this will be forthcoming when we discuss 3rd-party networking later.

• Internet Gateways cannot be used across a VPC peer link. This means that one VPC cannot send traffic to the Internet via another VPC's IGW. This will make more sense when we discuss Internet connectivity, but it is a common misconception about VPC peering and so it's addressed here.

• Route Tables will not be automatically updated with the CIDR of the peered VPC. Any routing to occur between natively peered VPCs needs to be set up in the main or custom Route Tables in the respective VPCs.

• VPC peers are not transitive. If VPC A peers to VPC B, and VPC B peers to VPC C, traffic cannot flow between VPC A and C, even if Route Tables are updated. This is because the VPC router is not actually routing packets in the data plane, the VPC peer attachment is an underlay connection between VPCs.

• In the above example, to get traffic between VPC A and VPC C, a separate VPC peer between A and C needs to be set up. This is a scaling issue as VPC peers can quickly scale to the maximum limit (referenced in a link in the appendix, as this may change), as well as being very annoying to administrate. It's a little like iBGP without the routing component, requiring a full mesh of neighbors to work correctly.

More details can be found on the AWS site regarding VPC Peering:

https://docs.aws.amazon.com/vpc/latest/peering/vpc-peering-basics.html

Let's look at an example of routing to VPC peers. In this example, we're setting up multiple Route Tables to demonstrate the way Route Tables can be customized or changed. Assume that LAN2 and LAN4 have similar restrictions as in previous examples, while LAN 1 and LAN3 are unrestricted.

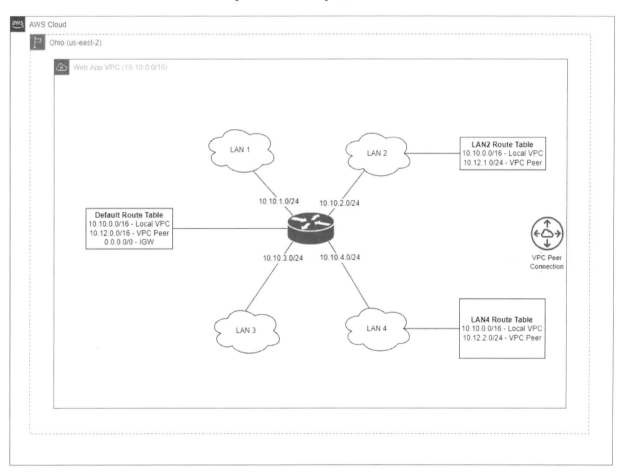

**Figure 16: Example VPC Peer Route Tables**

LAN 2 can communicate with any host in the local VPC, or LAN 1 (10.12.1.0/24) in the peered VPC. LAN 4 is similar but can communicate with LAN 2 (10.12.2.0/24) in the remote VPC instead. Here's what the LAN4 Route Table looks like.

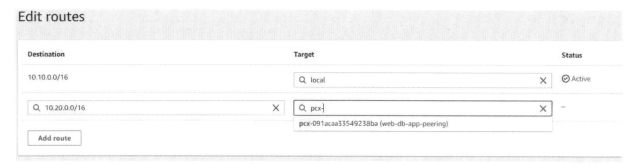

**Figure 17: Example RT for VPC Peer Routing**

Of course, in the other VPC, the Route Tables must be edited similarly so that return communication can take place, or the traffic will be dropped for lack of a return route.

All in all, VPC Peering is the least complex, but most manual and administratively involved method of sending traffic between VPCs. It requires a full mesh of VPCs as it is not transitive, it has a very low maximum number of peers, and it requires a massive amount of manual Route Table manipulation to be effective.

We move on from here to a topic that could probably be its own book entirely, the AWS Transit Gateway.

# Transit Gateway

The AWS Transit Gateway (TGW) is a managed routing/data plane service that's the closest cloud native service to what we network engineers are used to. It can handle dynamic routing, static routing, and it connects cloud native constructs together like a real router would. If we peel back the fabric, it's a managed virtual machine instance owned and operated by AWS. The Transit Gateway is a black box router for connecting AWS networks as well as 3rd-party devices together. It can peer BGP as well as terminate IPSEC and GRE tunnels, and, in fact, when you create a TGW you must supply a BGP ASN. These BGP ASNs can overlap with other TGWs, but it's really better that each TGW have its own.

The TGW is the hub in the AWS hub and spoke network architecture. It is instantiated outside of the VPC architecture and tied to a region. Because it's a managed service, it cannot be configured directly, though parts of it can be. Here's a basic network diagram of a TGW and a few VPCs for reference:

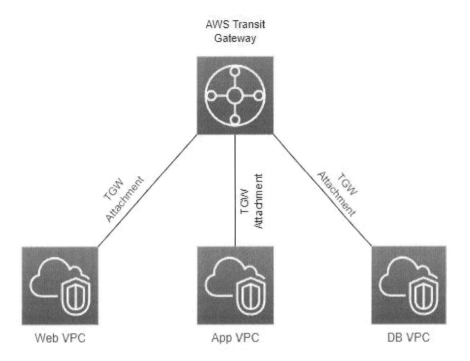

**Figure 18: Sample TGW Architecture**

A TGW can connect many VPCs together in a region, an order of magnitude beyond what is available with VPC Peering. Because a TGW is tied to a region, it can only attach VPCs in that region. To connect VPCs in different regions together via a TGW, a TGW can be spun up in another region and the two can be peered together.

Of course, there are limits to how much one can connect to a single TGW, or how many TGWs can be peered together. Since the cloud is an ever-changing landscape, any limits written down here are likely to be wrong by tomorrow morning. In the appendix, there will be links to check the AWS quotas. This can help when planning network deployments.

TGW Attachments are objects like the native VPC Peer attachments. This means that they are underlay fabric connections built by AWS to connect resources together. Because the TGW Attachment is an object, the VPC Route Tables can use the TGW Attachment as a destination for remote networks. When a Transit Gateway Attachment is created, there is actually an ENI placed in one or more selected subnets of the VPC. While only one ENI is needed to connect a VPC to a TGW, it's possible that multiple subnets may be attached to the TGW for redundancy in case one of the AZs fail. Here's an example:

**VPC attachment**
Select and configure your VPC attachment.

☑ DNS support  Info

☐ IPv6 support  Info

☐ Appliance Mode support  Info

VPC ID
Select the VPC to attach to the transit gateway.

| vpc-0dce4d60dba1b388e (WebApp-VPC) ▼ |

Subnet IDs  Info
Select the subnets in which to create the transit gateway VPC attachment.

☑ us-east-2a        | subnet-0ba1b7a73ff4cc06e (LAN1) ▼ |

☑ us-east-2b        | subnet-0509a07eae5db8677 (LAN4) ▼ |

☐ us-east-2c        No subnet available

| subnet-0ba1b7a73ff4cc06e ✕ |   | subnet-0509a07eae5db8677 ✕ |

Figure 19: TGW Attachment Creation

The TGW also has a main/default Route Table, just like VPCs. The TGW route table differs from that of a VPC route table because, by default, the CIDR ranges from attached VPC resources are automatically propagated to the TGW main Route Table. This means that while not exactly dynamic, the Route Table of a TGW is far easier to manage. In the reverse direction, the VPC Main Route Table can be populated by the TGW but does not have to be if route filtering is needed.

In fact, given the hub and spoke nature of TGW, and the fact that the TGW will (by default) know all the routes for remote destinations, VPCs can be treated as stub networks from a routing perspective. In cases where all remote destinations will use an RFC 1918 address, for example, the VPCs might only have RFC1918 supernet routes with the TGW attachment as the next hop.

This type of deployment is standard but by no means is it exhaustive. When we start talking about 3rd-party NVAs, for example, the routing can get very interesting. Imagine an Internet Gateway or virtual firewall in the VPC with the workloads (a term used to refer to compute tasks in the cloud, be they VMs or services) providing local Internet egress. The default route should point at that next hop, not a TGW attachment. But what if the TGW is attached to a VPC full of firewalls and the local VPC has none? In that case, a default route pointing at the TGW attachment makes sense so that traffic can be routed to a firewall VPC for Internet egress, just as an example.

It's important to note that TGW Attachments can also be configured with custom Route Tables. This affects the Transit Gateway routing decisions in the same ways that we've already discussed around custom subnet Route Tables in VPCs. We can restrict and customize the routing table for a particular attachment, meaning that the TGW can granularly make routing decisions. This is far closer to the traditional VRF construct than Subnet Route Tables are. In fact, TGW attachments can propagate the CIDRs for their attachments to their own or other Route Tables, whether it be the main/default Route Table for the TGW or other custom TGW Route Tables, just like MPLS VPN and route import/export. Here's an example:

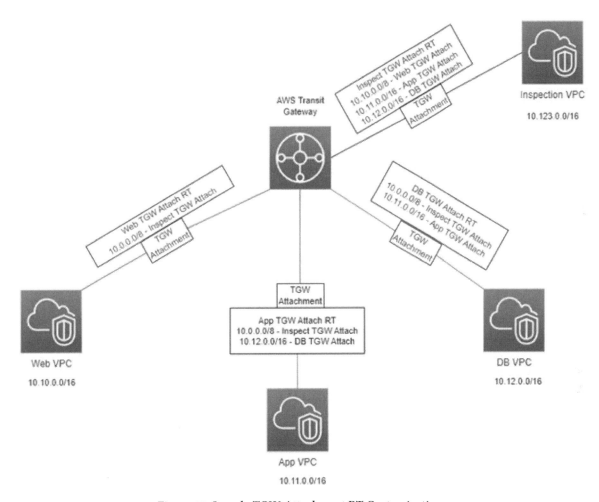

**Figure 20: Sample TGW Attachment RT Customization**

In this example, each TGW attachment has a customized Route Table. Through selective route propagation and static routing, the Web VPC cannot directly send traffic to the App and DB VPCs, or vice versa. Instead, the traffic will be routed by the Transit Gateway to the Inspection VPC where a security appliance waits to inspect traffic. The App and DB VPCs can communicate directly without need of the Inspection VPC because they are not exposed to the Internet. We are using the static 10.0.0.0/8 CIDR to force the traffic to the Inspect VPC, which has the specific routes to the other VPCs.

The TGW Attachment RT is consulted when traffic enters the attachment from a VPC. What that means is in the above scenario, for traffic leaving the App VPC, if the destination is 10.10.1.100, for example, the App TGW Attach RT uses the most specific route available, 10.0.0.0/8 to the Inspect VPC attachment. The traffic is delivered to the Inspection VPC across that attachment for inspection. Within the Inspection VPC itself is the subnet RT attached the TGW, which would need routes also pointing at a virtual firewall appliance or firewall service. The firewall appliance/service would inspect and return traffic to the VPC in an egress subnet with a different RT, pointing at the TGW attachment, as below:

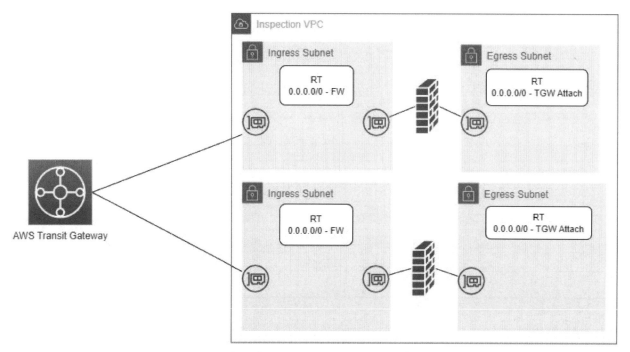

**Figure 21: Sample Inspection VPC/TGW Architecture**

Remember that there are multiple layers of routing happening here, starting with a packet at the workload level in the App VPC, the Subnet RT is consulted, directing the traffic to the TGW Attachment. Then the TGW Attachment RT is consulted as traffic hits that, and so on. When traffic is redirected to the firewall appliance or service,that must have its own RT to direct egress traffic to the proper subnet where it will be redirected back to the TGW Attachment. The Inspection TGW Attachment has the propagated CIDRs of all the attached VPCs, so it can direct the packet to its destination VPC.

Transit Gateway routing and its interaction with other AWS networking services could fill an entire book. We'll discuss the TGW more as we continue this journey through AWS cloud networking. Remember that the goal of this book is to be concise and get you speaking the language with understanding, not to become a TGW expert. There are plenty of resources available to really dig deep which will be linked in the appendix.

# PrivateLink

AWS PrivateLink is a technology we have already indirectly discussed, as it powers VPC peering and other ENI-based connectivity. What we will cover in this section has more to do with how you as an engineer can either provide a service to consumers or consume services from a provider like a private Software-as-a-Service (SaaS) connection.

PrivateLink powers a lot of AWS service-based connectivity but can also be leveraged by customers to provide cross-account private, non-Internet-based connectivity.

PrivateLink is a little like establishing a private tunnel (well, let's be real, it IS a private tunnel, you just don't control the tunnel itself) in that it provides connectivity between two endpoints using the AWS underlay.

Let's examine a use case and diagram for PrivateLink and it will make more sense:

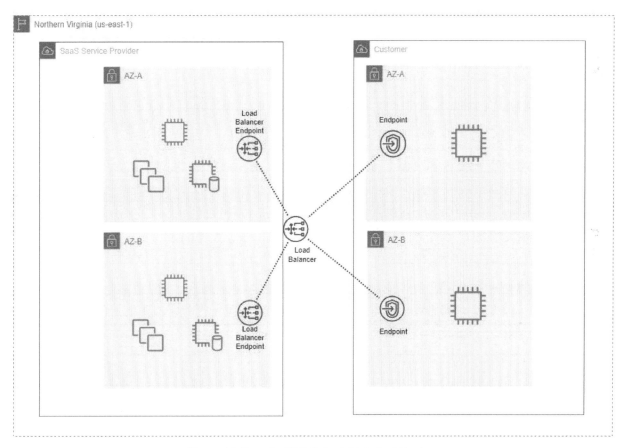

**Figure 22: Sample AWS PrivateLink Architecture**

In this diagram, we have a business offering some sort of service to customers, privately or via the AWS Marketplace. Customers can connect to their service offer using the AWS PrivateLink technology with Endpoints. Endpoints, like most network constructs, are just logical host tracking objects from a fabric perspective. It's an ENI, not to put too fine a point on it. The customer creates an endpoint in a subnet within the desired VPC and references the service:

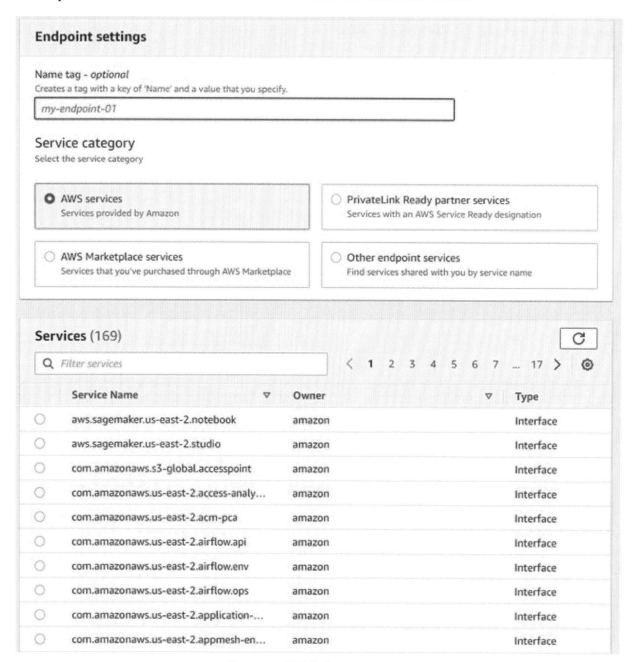

**Figure 23: AWS Endpoint Creation**

Creating this endpoint creates a connection between this Endpoint ENI and the load balancer that the provider creates to manage the connections. If you ARE the provider of services, you create the Endpoint service load balancer instead:

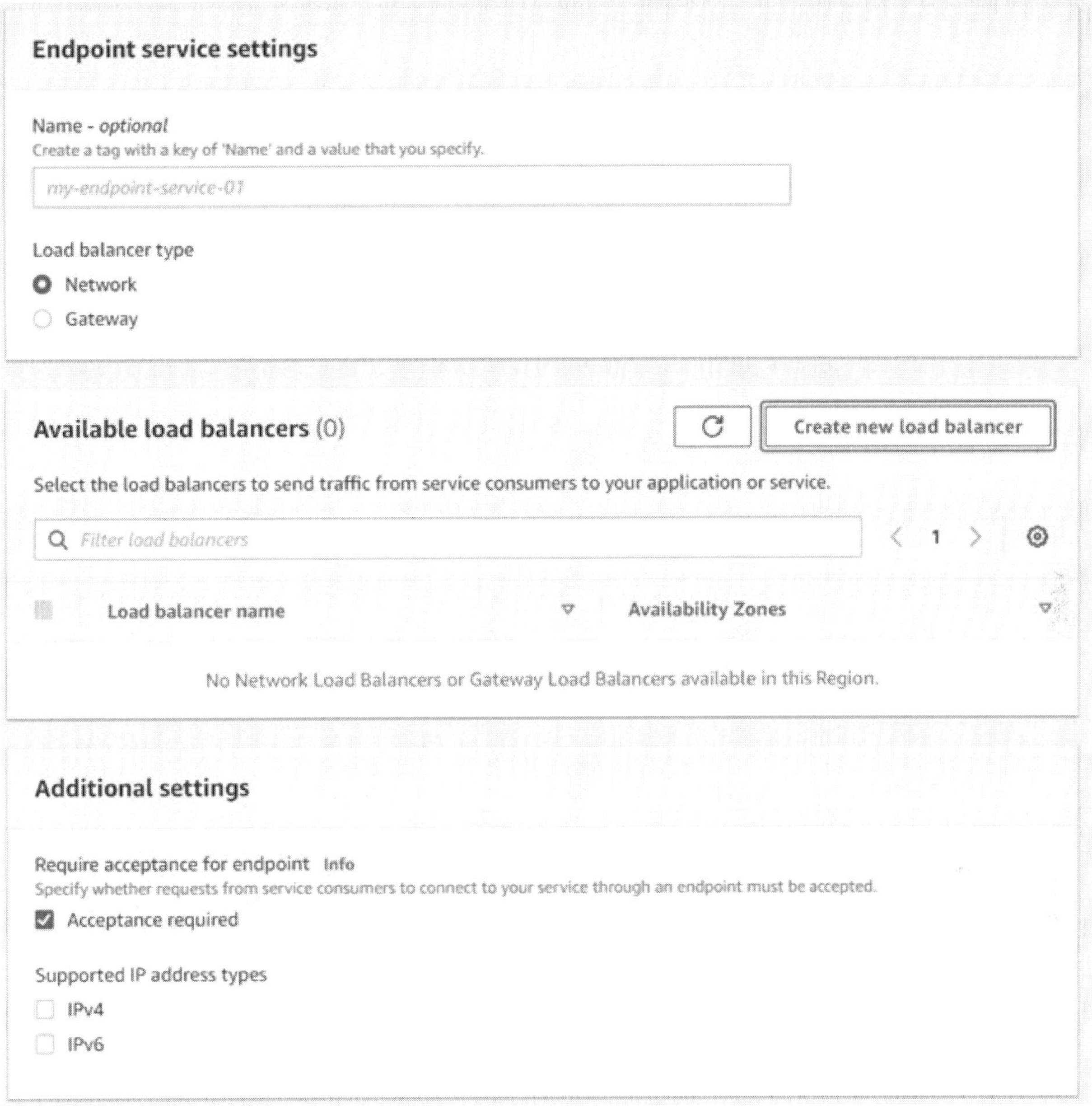

## Endpoint service settings

Name - *optional*
Create a tag with a key of 'Name' and a value that you specify.

> my-endpoint-service-01

Load balancer type

- ◉ Network
- ○ Gateway

## Available load balancers (0)

⟳  Create new load balancer

Select the load balancers to send traffic from service consumers to your application or service.

Q *Filter load balancers*    ‹  1  ›    ⚙

| ☐ | Load balancer name ▽ | Availability Zones ▽ |
|---|---|---|

No Network Load Balancers or Gateway Load Balancers available in this Region.

## Additional settings

Require acceptance for endpoint   Info
Specify whether requests from service consumers to connect to your service through an endpoint must be accepted.

- ☑ Acceptance required

Supported IP address types

- ☐ IPv4
- ☐ IPv6

**Figure 24: AWS Endpoint Service Creation**

From a network engineering perspective, what matters is this brings up a private tunnel between this instantiated Endpoint host and the service provider load balancer. What sort of services is this useful for, you ask? Well, many service providers offer cloud-ready data transformation services without having to build your own fleet of servers. You as the customer can simply consume the service rather than building your own. There are lots of possible services out there, but many enterprises ultimately don't want to manage fleets of services and would rather consume them from a business who is in the business of, well.. that business.

We haven't talked about Load Balancers yet, so I'm choosing to gloss over the options with Endpoint services for now. When we cover load balancing, we'll talk about the options there.

# Endpoints (Gateway, Interface)

We've talked about PrivateLink, the technology powering the endpoints, but let's spend a little time separating the Endpoints themselves from the technology. Endpoints can also give access to public AWS services to VPCs that lack an Internet Gateway, NAT Gateway, or other method of reaching the Internet to reach those services.

AWS has a LOT of services, and some of those services are 'public' services insofar as they can be accessed via the Internet (and some which must be). S3, the object storage service, is one such example. Normally to provide access to S3 buckets for file storage requires a VPC have Internet access to reach the S3 service. An Endpoint can obviate the need for Internet access to reach the service. It should be mentioned that Endpoints cannot be used to reach all AWS Public services, only supported ones.

Since the cloud changes constantly, the appendix will have a link to find the most recent services.

The biggest difference between the two options (Gateway and Interface) is best explained in list form.

Gateway Endpoints:

• Attach to a VPC itself, not any particular subnet

• Gateway Endpoints span AZs and are reachable via all subnets defined in a Prefix List

• Prefix List is used to automatically program subnet RT for those subnets to reach AWS services via the Gateway Endpoint, rather than updating RT statically

• Gateways are regional only, can't span across regions

• Gateway Endpoints only grant access from the VPC to which they are attached, peered VPCs cannot use the Gateway

Interface Endpoints:

• Connect to PrivateLink services

• Are an ENI and attach to a particular subnet, using an IP inside the range

• High availability requires more Endpoints in other subnets

• Limited protocol support (IPv4 and TCP)

• Routing to ENI is static as with other ENI-based services

• Accessing the service attached to the ENI is via DNS or IP. If using DNS, Interface Endpoint DNS entries are inserted into the VPC to redirect service calls to that endpoint

• This DNS behavior matters for private-only subnets that can not resolve the public DNS name of the service

The main takeaway from this entire section is that from a network engineering perspective, it's helpful to know the options to connect to 3rd-party or public AWS services from within private-only architectures. This is accomplished by the SDN automating a private-only connection in the underlay from a VPC to a service. Routing points your packets at the tunnel endpoint and AWS takes care of the rest.

# Network Virtual Appliances

Just like AWS Transit Gateway, this is a topic which will end up spanning multiple sections of this book because of how versatile and integrated it is with cloud networking. This section will focus on introducing the NVA concept and then how they can be used to facilitate AWS-to-AWS communication.

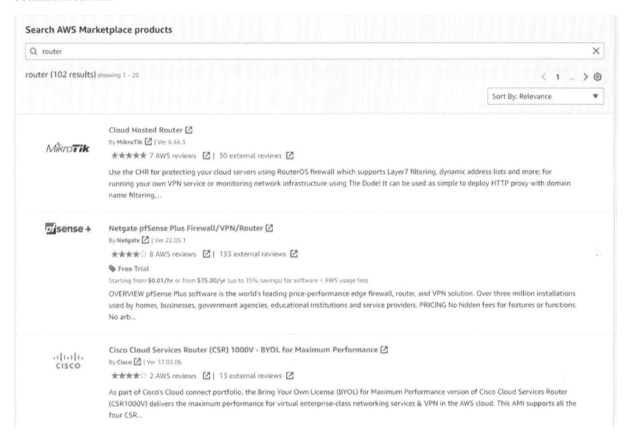

The AWS Marketplace is full of vendor offerings for virtual machines that can perform network functions. This is just a small slice of the possibilities. Of course, the idea of virtualized networking is in no way revolutionary. If anything, integrating virtual network appliances into the cloud is evolutionary. What's different now is how these NVAs can work with the native cloud constructs and deliver the granular networking capabilities you need. NVAs fill a role in cloud networking that goes beyond the basic options provided by the CSPs. They also provide familiar configuration options and peer well with on-prem devices that do things like dynamic routing at a deep level. Let's look at a sample architecture and what NVAs bring to the table over the native cloud options.

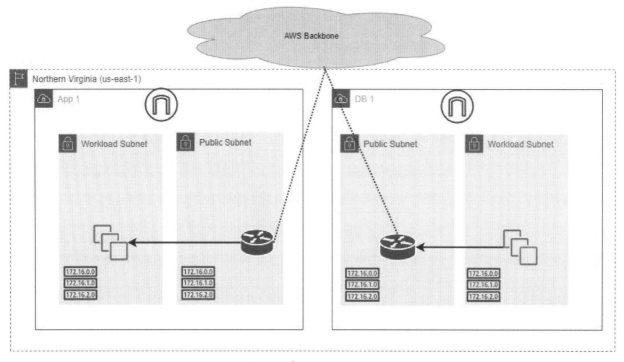

**Figure 25: Sample NVA Routing Pattern**

In this scenario we are providing routed connectivity between two workloads by using NVA Routers instead of VPC native peering or an AWS Transit Gateway. The routers establish an IPsec tunnel between them using the cloud architecture of subnets with an Internet Gateway. The NVA routers have their own routing table, and the traffic flow between workloads would look something like this:

1. Workload in the DB VPC workload subnet sends a packet to a workload in App VPC workload subnet via its default gateway (the VPC Router address, NOT the NVA router address)
2. The VPC uses the subnet Route Table to determine where to send this packet. Let's assume the subnet RT has a route pointing at the ENI of the NVA router.
3. The NVA router receives the packet and consults its own internal routing table, determining that the next hop is across the IPsec tunnel to the remote App VPC NVA Router.
4. The packet is encrypted in a tunnel with the next-hop address of the public IP of the NVA router in the App VPC, and the packet is then sent out of the interface to the local VPC.
5. The subnet Route Table of the public subnet uses the default route of the Internet Gateway.
6. At this point we're getting ahead of ourselves, since the next section is on Internet connectivity, but let's finish the explanation. It's okay if you are confused, we'll re-examine it in the next section.
7. The IGW performs a 1:1 static NAT for the public IP attached to the NVA router and sends the packet over the AWS backbone to the remote App VPC based on the destination IP address.

8. The remote IGW in the App VPC performs a 1:1 static NAT and delivers the encrypted packet to the NVA router, which decrypts the packet, consults its internal route table, and delivers the packet to the local subnet.
9. The subnet RT is consulted, and the packet is delivered to the local VPC workload.
10. When a reply happens, this all goes in reverse.

Now this is a very simplistic use case for NVA, but we need to start small and just understand the basic integration between an NVA and native cloud routing. Generally, we use the NVAs to overcome cloud limitations, create our own data plane, and give granular non-native control over the data. For example, OSPF and EIGRP are not supported by any cloud constructs, but if we create tunnels between two routers that do support those protocols, we could run them. The cloud native Route Tables would not even need to know about the routes being exchanged, because they would essentially become our new underlay for tunnels. Thus, they would only need enough routing to establish tunnels between the NVA routers.

In practice, we shouldn't just build the same network we use on-prem in the cloud. Those NVAs cost money to run, and so the reason for using NVAs needs to be more justified than simply wanting to use what's familiar. The main reason to create your own data plane in the cloud is to get visibility into the workload traffic by owning that data plane. Visibility is tough using native constructs, though there is basic visibility into traffic, any real visibility costs money.

# Connecting AWS Networks to the Internet

We've brushed up against Internet connectivity a few times up until this point, but we haven't had a good chance to learn how it works in AWS yet. In this section we'll talk about the different options for connecting VPCs and workloads to the Internet and what possibilities and limitations exist.

## Internet Gateway

The Internet Gateway has been mentioned several times now and now it's time to dig in. Prepare to be underwhelmed by the glory that is the Internet Gateway. Are you ready?

The Internet Gateway (IGW) is an object that attaches to a VPC, not a subnet, and provides Internet access for anything in the VPC that has public IP addresses. The IGW is, like most native cloud managed connectivity, just a host entry in the fabric tied to underlay architecture. In traditional networking terms, an IGW acts like a provider-managed edge router. That router has some upstream connectivity to the Internet and the 'LAN' side of that IGW is attached to the VPC. IGWs are redundant within a region and each VPC can have just one IGW associated. The IGW itself cannot be configured or addressed. It serves as a target for the subnet Route Tables in the VPC for traffic destined to the Internet.

The IGW does perform a very important function with public IP addresses assigned to workloads in the VPC, and that is to set up a static 1:1 NAT for the public IP to the private IP of the ENI of that workload. When traffic leaves or returns from the private IP of that workload the IGW will do the static NAT for it, making it accessible from the Internet. Though we haven't gotten there yet, the public IP is called an Elastic IP. More on that in a bit.

One other thing we can do with an IGW is create what's called an Edge Association. This allows us to create a custom Route Table for the IGW itself and assign it as an Edge Association, so that traffic coming from the Internet could be sent to a different destination than the VPC Router. Why would we do that? Here's an example of where such a solution would **not** be needed:

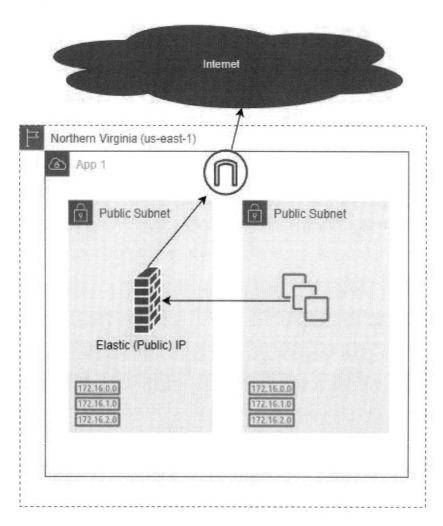

**Figure 26: IGW Egress Use Case**

If the workload in the public subnet is using the firewall for egress, the firewall will NAT the workload IP to its own IP address, then send the traffic to the IGW. When traffic returned from the Internet, the destination would be the firewall IP, ensuring symmetry in traffic flow. But what if it was like this?

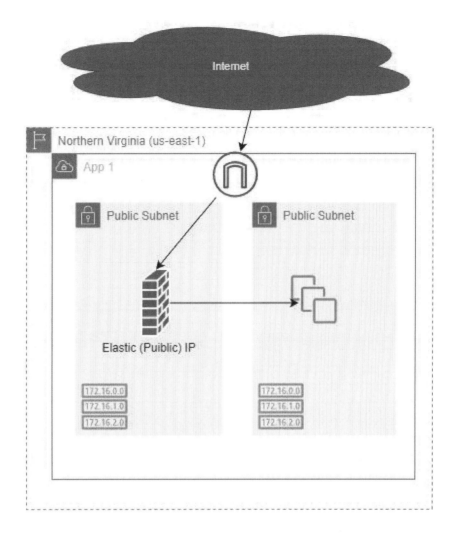

**Figure 27: IGW Ingress Use Case**

What if the goal was to provide security for a public workload? If the firewall only inspected traffic, but did not provide a NAT, what would happen when the IGW got traffic from the Internet destined to the public IP of the workload?

By default, the IGW returns traffic to the VPC router to make routing decisions, and this would result in the firewall being skipped for ingress traffic flows from the Internet. The answer here is to configure an IGW Edge Association so that the next-hop is the firewall ENI, then let the firewall route the traffic (if allowed) to the IP of the workload (covered next).

Importantly, the IGW itself provides Internet access but does not perform any NAT for local workloads lacking Elastic IPs. This means that the IGW is like a provider edge router that just offers Internet connectivity and expects you to have some other way to handle public IP addressing, whether that be static assignment of a public IP to each workload, or some device to do a NAT Overload / PAT.

The Internet Gateway also offers absolutely zero security on its own. The use of an IGW assumes that the VPC should be accessible from the Internet. The IGW comes with no firewall or rules to inspect inbound or outbound traffic, so any device within the VPC with a public IP will be publicly accessible via IGW. There are, of course, plenty of security measures to solve this that we will cover later, but it's important to understand the IGW itself offers no protection. Devices without a public IP associated are, of course, inaccessible from the Internet, and cannot access the Internet via the IGW without a public IP, but workloads with public IP associations that can reach the Internet are reachable in turn, which is why it is common to see public workloads protected by a virtual firewall appliance or service.

# Elastic IP

Elastic IP is kind of strange to us network engineers, but at this point in the book it shouldn't seem odd. Just like the Elastic Network Interface, an Elastic IP is a host tracking entry in the AWS fabric. This allows it to be associated with virtual machines (specifically ENIs) and moved as needed.

Let's look at a sample setup for a VPC that has a publicly accessible web server in a Web VPC with an IGW and the associated Elastic IP for the server:

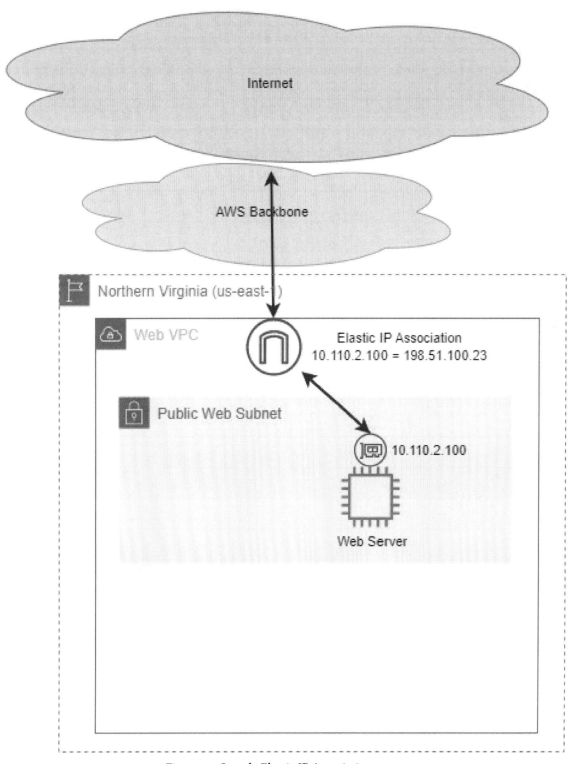

**Figure 28: Sample Elastic IP Association**

In this example, the web server has received an Elastic IP association pulled from the AWS pool of public IP addresses in the region. The Elastic IP (in the example, 198.51.100.23, which is not an actual AWS address, by the way) has been associated with the web server.

This part is important: The web server has no awareness of this public IP. The association is not the same thing as statically assigning the IP to the host. What the Elastic IP really does is create a static 1:1 NAT on the IGW within the VPC in which the ENI to which it is associated resides.

In traditional terms, this would be like having your provider set up a 1:1 static NAT on its router for a particular server, firewall, etc, to use a specific public address. The hosts behind that provider edge router would be unaware of the public IP, but the provider router would be performing the NAT and translating traffic to or from the associated public IP to the private IP of the host. Remember that this functionality comes with no protections. The IGW will merely translate the traffic to and from the host's private and public address for traffic to and from the Internet.

You CAN Bring Your Own IP to AWS if you want to do that. There are a lot of steps far outside the scope of this book that boil down to, "I give permission for AWS to announce these routes for me to attract traffic to these IPs". The functionality of using these IPs is the same.

The EIP must be associated to an ENI, but if an instance only has a single ENI, it can be defaulted to an instance association as below:

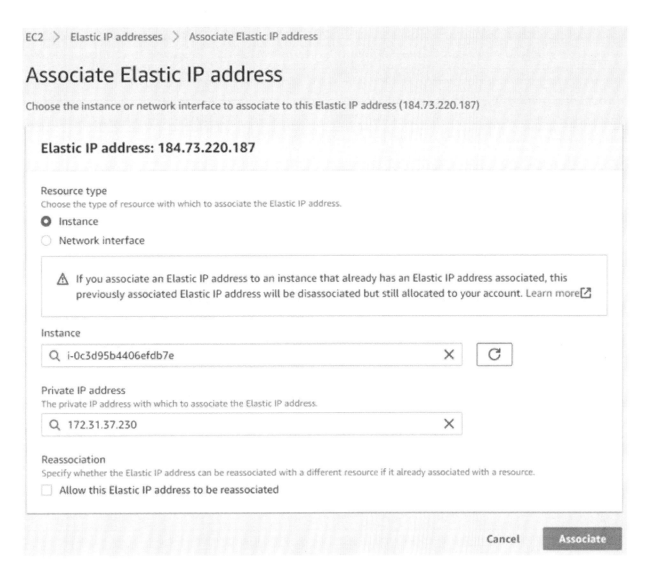

As shown, the EIP must match an instance ID / ENI ID, and map to a private IP in the VPC. This is how AWS knows on which IGW to place the 1:1 NAT entry for the EIP address.

# Egress-Only Internet Gateway

There are challenges faced by using IPv6 in the public cloud that can't be ignored. IPv6 addresses are, of course, globally routable by default, which can pose problems for workloads and VPCs built with IPv6 that want to be able to access the Internet but don't want the Internet to access them in turn.

The Egress-Only Internet Gateway (EIGW) aims to solve for this by introducing an IPv6-specific Internet Gateway. While IPv4 hosts can take advantage of native or NVA-based NAT services, IPv6 generally does not. The EIGW allows IPv6-based AWS workloads to access the Internet in an inside-out only fashion without having to use IPv6 NAT techniques, if those techniques are undesirable.

This is accomplished by adding an EIGW to a VPC and then adding a route pointing to the EIGW for the subnets where IPv6 workloads need outbound Internet access. The EIGW can be added alongside an IGW or NAT Gateway (which we will cover shortly) but only function for IPv6-addressed hosts.

The EIGW is something of an oddity, but it solves a very specific issue with securing IPv6 workloads when hosts need access to the Internet, are technically publicly addressed, and need to be secured from Internet attacks without front-ending the VPC with firewalls.

# NAT Gateway

NAT Gateway is an AWS service that a lot of people use for IPv4-based or IPv6-based workloads (For IPv6 workloads, it uses NAT64). It's a managed NAT service that keeps cloud developers from having to run their own NAT NVA instance (firewall, router, etc) to perform a NAT for them. The NAT Gateway can perform public or private NAT depending on where it is placed and what traffic is directed through it. The most common use is to allow Internet access for private hosts, but it can also translate IPv6 to IPv4 (and vice versa) or some other uses cases where a private NAT would be useful. Let's discuss the Internet use case and then the private one.

To support the Internet connectivity use case, the NAT Gateway must be placed into a public subnet (ie, a subnet with a default route to an IGW) to provide Internet access for private hosts. It must also be assigned an Elastic IP for use as the public IP. This is not surprising, under the covers, AWS is managing a NAT instance for you and that instance needs an Elastic IP address to reach the Internet just as your own instance would.

Here's a sample VPC architecture including a NAT Gateway to provide Internet access for private workloads, along with a public subnet with a web server that uses its own Elastic IP and does not need the NAT Gateway for reference:

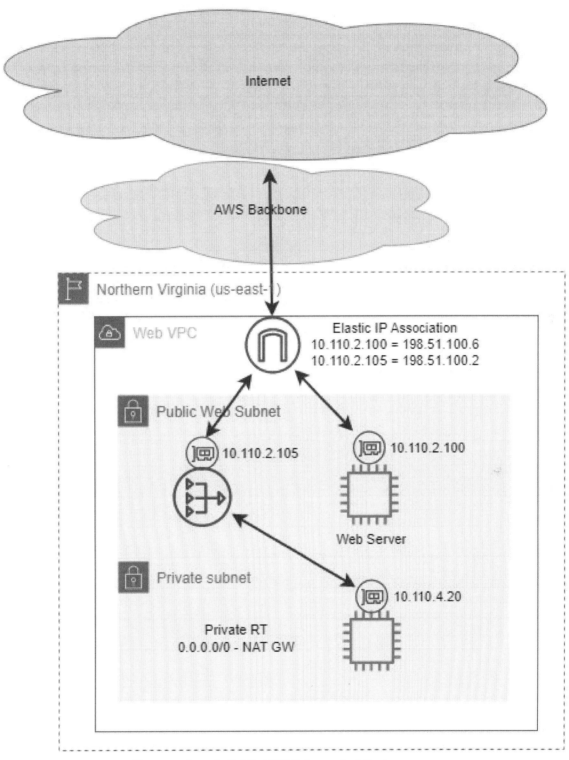

**Figure 29: Sample Public NAT Gateway Architecture**

Moving on, in the case of a private NAT Gateway, no Elastic IP is required. However, the use case for private NAT Gateway is complicated enough to make you run for your own NVA NAT instance. Let's look at how one might use NAT Gateway to solve an overlapping private IP issue.

Imagine two VPCs with identical IP addressing due to shadow IT and historical development efforts from two different business units. Now the time has come to integrate them via the network, and the problem is evident. The correct answer is to use a private NAT Gateway, a Load Balancer, and non-overlapping routable address space to front-end the connectivity, as shown:

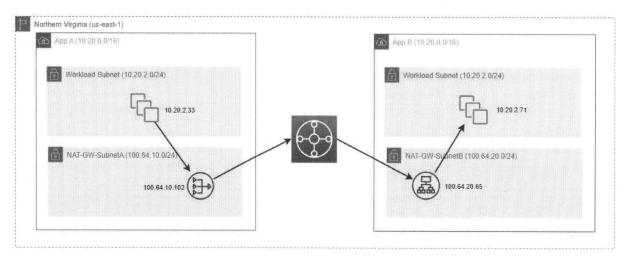

**Figure 30: Sample Private NAT Gateway Use Case**

But wait, you may be thinking, those arrows only point one way!

Yes, this use case is a one-way NAT. This is not a double or reverse NAT type of use case. If you need to do the same in reverse, you need different subnets, NAT Gateways, Load Balancers and Route Tables.

Here is how the overlapping NAT works in one direction. Keep in mind that a flow initiated from App B to App A in this example needs new subnets, new NAT Gateways, Load Balancers and Route Tables to work.

1. Packet leaves workload A destined to 100.64.20.25 (The NAT IP of a workload in App B VPC) with source IP 10.20.2.33
2. Subnet Route Table directs traffic for 100.64.20.0/24 to NAT Gateway in the other subnet
3. NAT GW performs a source NAT, changing the source IP of the packet from 10.20.2.33 to 100.64.10.102, destination is unchanged
4. NAT GW Subnet RT points traffic for destination IP 100.64.20.0/24 to Transit Gateway
5. Transit Gateway RT has only static routes between 100.64.10.0/24 and 100.64.20.0/24, NOT the 10.x addresses. The TGW delivers the packet to the Load Balancer subnet in VPC App B via its TGW attachment.
6. We haven't covered Load Balancers yet, but in this case the LB is going to perform a destination NAT (ie, change the packet's destination IP of 100.64.20.25 to 10.20.2.71)
7. The LB will also source NAT the traffic, so that the source IP is not 100.64.10.102 but 100.64.20.65 (itself)

8. Packet is delivered to workload B.
9. If Workload B responds, the LB will change the source IP from Workload B to itself (100.64.20.65) and destination IP will be the one in its session table, 100.64.10.102, the NAT GW address in App A.
10. Traffic flows through the TGW based on the TGW RT and attachments back to App A NAT GW, which checks its own NAT session table, and changes the destination IP from 100.64.10.102 (itself) to the original Workload A IP of 10.20.2.33.

Not complicated at all, right?

NAT Gateways come with restrictions, and they also come with charges. In addition to the NAT Gateway charge simply for having it, there is also an associated data transfer cost. There is a maximum data rate limit, maximum session limit, and NAT Gateways are also only redundant within a single AZ. This means that if you want NAT Gateway redundancy in different availability zones, you must have multiple NAT Gateways. VPC Peering does not allow the use of a NAT Gateway in the peered VPC, the same as an IGW. VPC Peering only allows connectivity between the two VPCs, and not the use of VPC-attached services. The link to the details will be in the appendix as these are constantly in flux.

# Network Virtual Appliances

We just talked about some cloud native limitations, such as the inability of a VPC peer structure to utilize a peered Internet Gateway. NVAs extend the functionality of cloud architectures by allowing you to make your own rules. The NVAs themselves still must conform to the rules of the cloud, but you can create your own data plane on top of it and introduce functionality more granularly.

Consider:

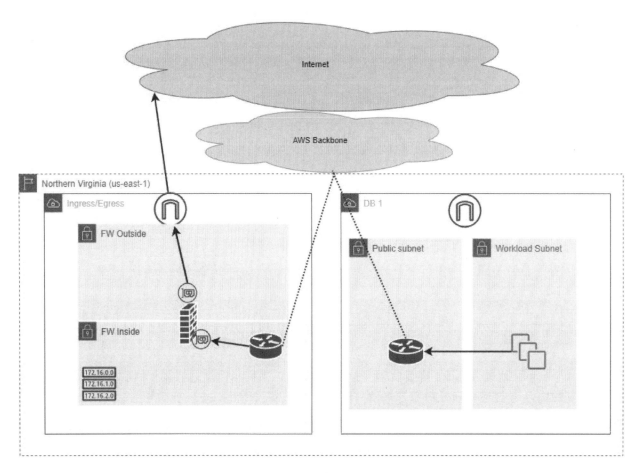

Above, we have a private workload subnet that should not have direct access to the Internet. It's highly unlikely that would be the only VPC in production with this requirement, so we establish a VPC solely for the purpose of centralizing ingress and egress traffic. The private workloads have an NVA in the VPC, some sort of routing platform. The private subnet of the VPC will use the ENI of the router as its next-hop for default traffic. That router will have a standard routing configuration. There are multiple options on what could happen next, and it's only limited by the connectivity the NVA can leverage.

In the example, this router creates a data plane tunnel over the native cloud architecture to another router NVA in the VPC with a firewall. The integrity, confidentiality and authenticity of this data can be maintained by using encrypted tunneling. The underlying cloud native subnets and Route Tables only need to provide connectivity between the two NVAs using the AWS backbone. The NVAs use public IP addressing to establish this tunnel, so technically this is public traffic, using the Internet Gateways, but it is not routed over the Internet itself in this case.

When traffic from the private workload reaches the NVA router in the Ingress/Egress VPC, the router follows its own route table and dumps the traffic into the local subnet. The local cloud native subnet Route Table needs to send default traffic to the ENI of the firewall NVA's inside/LAN interface. The firewall itself has a routing table and inspection rules and will perform a NAT and send Internet-bound traffic out to its public ENI, where it will egress via the Internet Gateway.

The Internet Gateway has the 1:1 NAT setup for the elastic IP address attached to the firewall public ENI and performs its own NAT, sending the traffic to the Internet. On return, the traffic flows in reverse.

This is just one of a ton of possibilities to provide Internet access via NVAs. The main thing to keep in mind is that to reach the Internet, even NVAs must use the cloud native constructs that provide that access. They can have an Elastic IP or use a NAT gateway (the NVA can NAT and then the NAT Gateway can NAT the private address of the NVA, on down the line), but NVAs also vastly extend the possibilities of granularity and control concerning the NAT itself, not to mention visibility into the traffic, NAT tables and sessions.

# Connecting AWS Networks to Other Networks

Throughout this book, we've discussed cloud networking topics in enough detail to have a good conversation about cloud networking without needing to become an expert. Now, we need to dive slightly deeper than the previous topics, because for network engineers, it will be the hybrid networking that defines where most non-cloud engineers will have to integrate with cloud networks. That means understanding the integration options and choices at a deeper level.

If you've made it this far you have a good understanding of how cloud networking works generally, and some of the constructs that are available to move packets. Now it's time to strap on the scuba gear and go deeper, but only for this section. Where on-prem networks need to integrate with cloud networks is where you must be stronger, and we'll need to spend the extra effort.

## Customer Gateway / Virtual Gateway

The way AWS handles Site to Site IPsec VPN is standard, but it's wrapped in an MSP-like experience. As mentioned all the way at the beginning, a CSP is an MSP, and all MSPs expose only the limited feature sets they allow you to use. What that means is setting up IPsec S2S VPN is not unusual or difficult, it's just on rails.

There are a lot of details around what is and isnt supported from a VPN perspective and they keep changing, so some of this will involve a bit of hand waving and referral to links in the appendix. We will go deeper on the architecture and routing instead. From a Customer Gateway / Virtual Private Gateway Site to Site VPN perspective, it's just an IPsec tunnel configuration. You set up the AWS side and you specify how your side (on-prem firewall, router, etc) is configured, and AWS will automatically configure its side for the IPsec connection. If your device is supported for it, AWS also supplies the configurations to use for the on-prem side of the connection. The actual architecture of a typical S2S VPN looks like this:

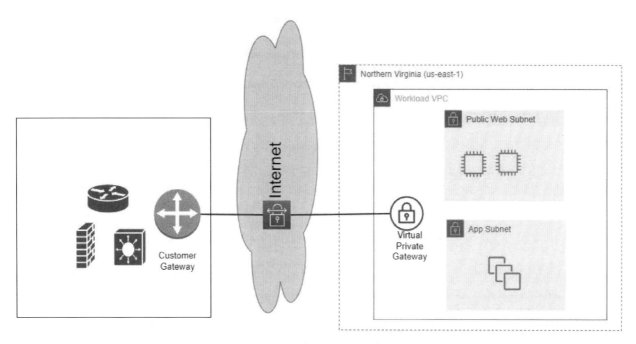

**Figure 31: Typical S2S VPN Architecture**

Remember that a CSP is an MSP, and let's look at some of the options given to us to set this up. The CGW doesn't exist in the cloud, of course, it is a representation of the remote endpoint on-prem.

# Create customer gateway Info

A customer gateway is a resource that you create in AWS that represents the customer gateway device in your on-premises network.

## Details

**Name tag - *optional***
Creates a tag with a key of 'Name' and a value that you specify.

```
CGW1
```

Value must be 256 characters or less in length.

**BGP ASN** Info
The ASN of your customer gateway device.

```
65100
```

Value must be in 1 - 2147483647 range.

**IP address** Info
Specify the IP address for your customer gateway device's external interface.

```
20.68.222.19
```

**Certificate ARN**
The ARN of a private certificate provisioned in AWS Certificate Manager (ACM).

```
Select certificate ARN                                          ▼
```

**Device - *optional***
Enter a name for the customer gateway device.

```
Enter device name
```

As you can see, regarding the on-prem side, the options are fairly light. We can set a BGP ASN, the remote end IP address, and whether we are using a certificate for authentication. When we go to create the AWS side of things, we'll refer to this CGW object. Let's do that now and see what the VGW setup looks like. Remember that a VGW is a tracked host object endpoint that can terminate multiple VPN tunnels. Here's the VGW creation. Again, there's very little to be done here.

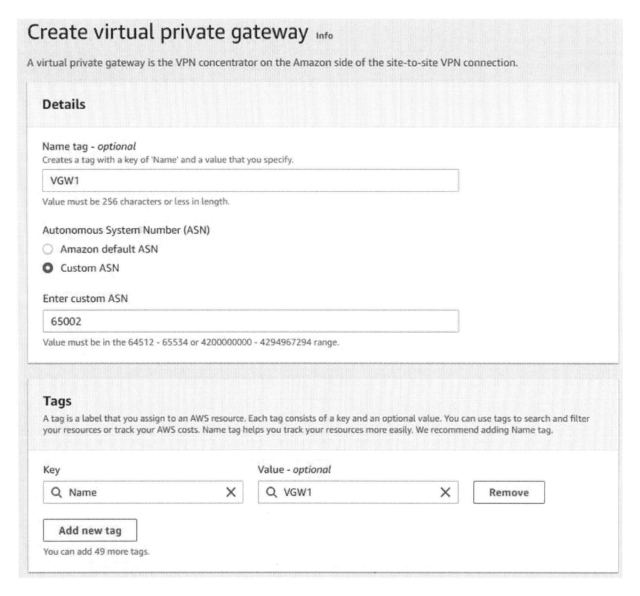

Notice that besides setting an ASN and a name you can't do anything else. The VGW does nothing by itself; it must be attached to a VPC to be used. VGWs are region-specific and can only be attached to one VPC, but it can be moved between VPCs within the same region. It is AZ-redundant within a region and does not attach to any subnet. Once we attach the VGW to a VPC, we can create the Site-to-Site VPN. Here's what the setup looks like:

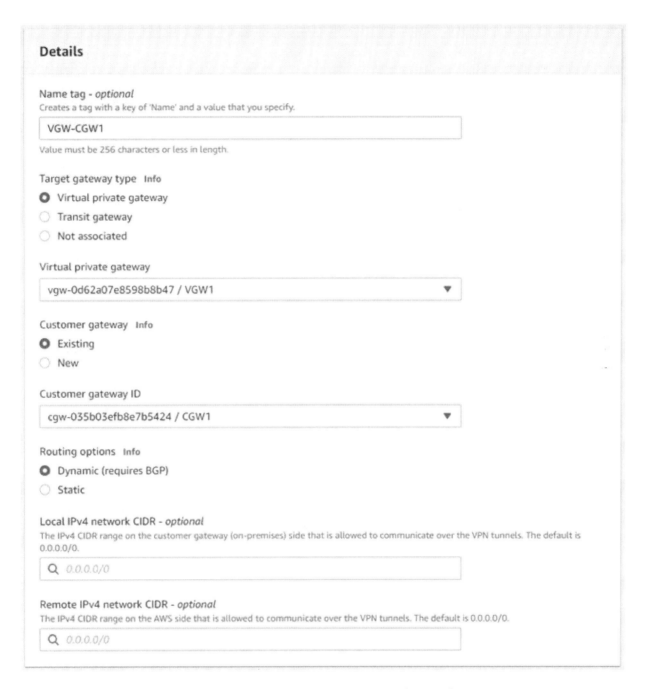

We can use BGP or stick to static routing. We can also restrict what prefixes can communicate across the tunnel if needed. In this case we are using BGP, but if static routing is selected then the VGW creates static routes in the VPC RT for the selected prefixes instead of learning what to program via BGP.

The VGW setup creates two tunnels for redundancy in different AZs, each tunnel can be configured with extra options. Visibility is always a problem in the cloud because so little of the architecture is exposed, but here AWS gives us the option to log VPN activity to CloudWatch, the AWS logging system. After creating the VPN connection, we can download the configuration to apply so long as it is a supported device. In this case it's a CSR1000v.

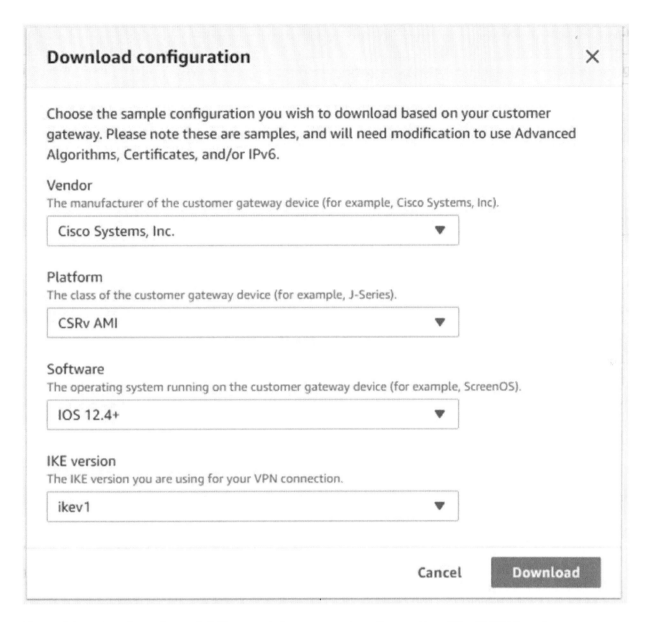

From this point, the only real difference is how you set up the routing. The VGW does have an upper limit of BGP prefixes it can accept. The limit is VERY low, but the appendix will have links to the current details.

This sort of limitation is a result of hyperscale. Hyperscale is a term we haven't discussed yet, but you can imagine how difficult it is to create an SDN that can handle millions of tenants and their specific network requirements. Hyperscalers (CSPs in this case) can scale only because their loads are manageable. If the fabric control planes, even separated, had to account for thousands of routes per tenant, using very simple constructs like a VGW, it would not scale. AWS does have an offering that can scale to more routes in the Transit Gateway, but the VGW is a simple construct. A Transit Gateway is a dedicated AWS-managed virtual appliance. The VGW is little more than an SDN object.

These limitations will impact your network design and it's very important to be aware of them, as well as the cost associated with managing the design. A VGW costs a lot less than a Transit Gateway but supports a lot less. These limitations matter as you try to scale your cloud network, as well as integrate with the on-prem networks in a hybrid way.

Not to veer too far off the path, but let's briefly talk about how you overcome these sorts of limitations if the architecture requires a VGW attachment instead of something smarter. Perhaps the S2S VPN is all that's needed in the beginning or maybe the business can't justify something more expensive, with better routing support. How will you meet the need while staying within the boundaries?

The short answer is the best one: It depends.

If you can summarize prefix advertisements to the cloud, you should always do so. Especially for enterprises who have large on-prem footprints who only started moving to cloud recently, it's highly likely that the cloud space is smaller and uses less prefixes, hopefully with more contiguous blocks of IPs. This allows you to summarize advertisements from on-prem to the cloud, possibly reducing the entire advertisement to one prefix, the supernet of your private addressing schema (like 10.0.0.0/8).

If the business is using some SaaS offer, and cloud resources need to access it, try to avoid advertising the SaaS prefixes from on-prem to the cloud. Let cloud resources use cloud Internet if possible, this saves thousands of prefixes from needing to be advertised to cloud resources.

We'll cover more design principles as we further explore the extracloud-to-cloud connectivity options. The CGW/VGW connection using S2S VPN is probably the simplest implementation (and most familiar).

# AWS Direct Connect

What to do when you need private connectivity from an on-prem location all the way to AWS? Is there a way to get a private dedicated circuit for AWS connectivity? Yes. The answer is yes. How we accomplish this is arguably the most familiar part of cloud networking you'll run into: The Direct Connect, or DX. It involves some connectivity to a 3rd party colo/data center, physical rack cabling, a cross-connect, and 802.1q encapsulation.

Here's a typical Direct Connect setup:

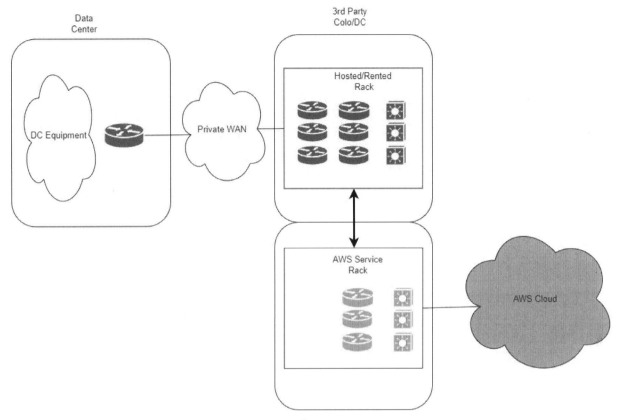

**Figure 32: Typical AWS Direct Connect**

AWS offers connectivity to their cloud via dedicated physical cabling at an AWS-partnered facility. Sometimes the AWS gear is connected directly at the facility and other times it is just terminating a dedicated circuit on some sort of bank of ports, like a switch. The above diagram assumes that AWS has a presence at a 3rd-party dedicated hosting facility, and that an AWS customer that wants to leverage a Direct Connect will buy the DX port from AWS and have that port physically cabled across racks/cages to the customer equipment (if deployed), or a provider router to feed to a customer on-prem connection.

The Direct Connect itself is just a physical port on AWS infrastructure that connects back to the AWS fabric through their deployed network hardware. A physical cable is extended via an authorized technician (not you) to an endpoint in the facility. That connectivity is between AWS and the customer, which either picks up that connectivity from their own router deployed in a rack, or gets it extended over some sort of provider to the customer endpoint. For the purposes of this example, let's assume the most common setup, that a customer is purchasing some sort of connectivity from a service provider to be extended to their data center. Let's cover the physical requirements when connecting to a Direct Connect, now that we understand what it's for:

• 1, 10, or 100Gbps speed (providers can subdivide/fractionalize this)

• DX Handoff is SM Fiber, not copper, use the correct SFPs for the speeds required

• Manual, not autonegotiation, for speed and duplex

• BGP is the only supported protocol and must use MD5 authentication

• MTU 1500 supported, 9100 supported on Private VIF only, 8500 for Transit VIF only

• DX does support BFD and MACsec if you want to use these

Some of these physical characteristics matter a great deal if the AWS DX handoff is direct to your equipment at the DX location. If a provider is handling that part and extending it to you, of course, the provider's physical requirements are what matter. The DX itself is just, at the end of the day, a Layer 2 circuit trunking VLANs. The VLANs are based on what choose to deploy on your DX. and that's what we'll talk about next: The Virtual Interface, or VIF, and all its flavors. VIFs are basically VLANs that give access to different areas of the AWS cloud or offer different connectivity. AWS charges a fee for having a DX and a data egress charge. Traffic into AWS is free, but traffic leaving AWS is subject to a charge. In another life, the founders of AWS must have ran a moderately successful (though bizarre) hotel in California and carried over the operating model.

## AWS DX – Private VIF

Virtual Interface sounds so much cooler and cloudier than VLAN, but here we are. The AWS DX is a trunk and we have the ability to split out that trunk into multiple types of VIFs. These VIFs do different things, and as you may have already guessed, the Private VIF is focused on connecting your on-prem services to your AWS cloud VPC environments in a private way. Rather than needing to set up VPN connectivity over an untrusted network, the Private VIF gives privacy (at the VLAN level) without the need for encryption. This means the data transfer rate can be higher and with less overhead, so long as the organization allows unencrypted (but private) connectivity between on-prem and AWS. Otherwise, it's likely that MACsec or an IPSec tunnel on top of the DX will be needed.

There are several options to terminate the logical side of the AWS cloud connection. Each VIF type provides connectivity in the same physical way, but logically different. The Private VIF provides logical connectivity between the customer side of the DX and the customer VPC side of AWS via BGP peering over the VLAN. Without using a DX Gateway (coming up) or Transit VIF (coming up), a private VIF connects to a Virtual Private Gateway in a single VPC within the same AWS region.

Here's what a normal Private VIF connection looks like, attached to a VGW in a single VPC:

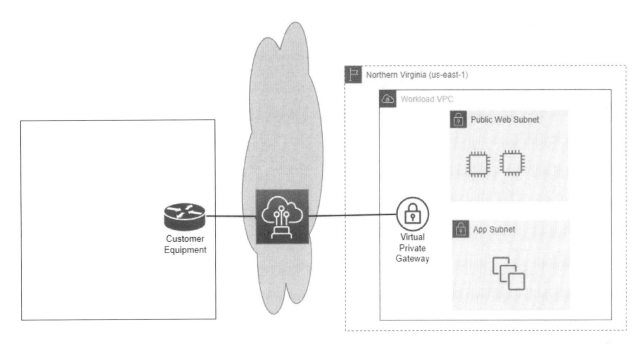

**Figure 33: Basic Private VIF w/ DX**

The physical deployment is as we covered earlier, but from a logical perspective, a private VIF will just be a BGP neighborship set up over a VLAN/dot1q interface. One side will be the customer equipment and the other will be the VGW. The VGW can be set to propagate routes learned via the customer side into the main VPC Route Table or not as desired. The VPC CIDR is advertised to the customer side as well. This setup is very simple and not very scalable, but it does work. Remember that a DX is region-locked, and Private VIF connectivity only works within that same region, but you can have multiple Private VIFs connected to different VPCs via VGW. Another important limitation to point out is that the VGW can only accept a small number of prefixes from the on-prem side. The exact number will be in the AWS docs linked in the appendix but expect it to stay artificially small. Let's move on to the Public VIF.

## AWS DX – Public VIF

The Public VIF is far more interesting than the Private VIF. The basic technology is the same, it's a dedicated VLAN on the DX, but instead of connecting to your AWS VPC environment, it allows access to the AWS public services and public IPs such as S3 Object Storage, AWS Lambda, etc. This connectivity uses the AWS backbone, not the Internet, but it is a public connection. Because of this, it does not allow you to connect to resources with private IPs, such as VPC-based virtual devices and services. Technically it is possible to do so with CGW/VGW, but it seems somewhat silly to ride a private circuit to the public side of AWS just to establish a VPN to the private resources. Just use a Private VIF.

A Public VIF must be set up with public IP addressing on the customer side, and AWS will allocate its own public IP addresses on the peer side. There are a few options how to get the customer-side public address, depending on what the customer can provide:

• Customer-owned IPv4 CIDR. Unlike on the Internet, you don't have to advertise a /24 CIDR

• If using a partner/provider, they must provide an authorization document to use their public IP (https://aws.amazon.com/vpc/faqs/#Bring_Your_Own_IP)

• AWS has a limited amount of their own public IPs that can be allocated, this is on a best-effort basis

• If using IPv6 AWS will handle the allocation, you can not specify your own address for peering.

There are several ways to customize the Public VIF experience using BGP as well. When setting up the BGP peering with AWS over the Public VIF, you can use your organization's Public BGP ASN if desired, or a small subset of Private ASN options.

Using your organizations public BGP ASN allows you to do things like AS-PATH prepending if advertising prefixes you own, which can be helpful with traffic preference if you have multiple DX connections. If using a private ASN, the advertisement cannot be modified. AWS will, by default, advertise ALL the AWS region IPs over the Public VIF to the on-prem peer. This allows you to connect with other region's public services if needed, since the DX will advertise all the public IPs over BGP to the on-prem infrastructure. It could be that this is undesirable, however, and so AWS also supports BGP communities to allow filtering of routes geographically.

Let's look at a sample Public VIF connection and how the routes are being advertised to and from AWS.

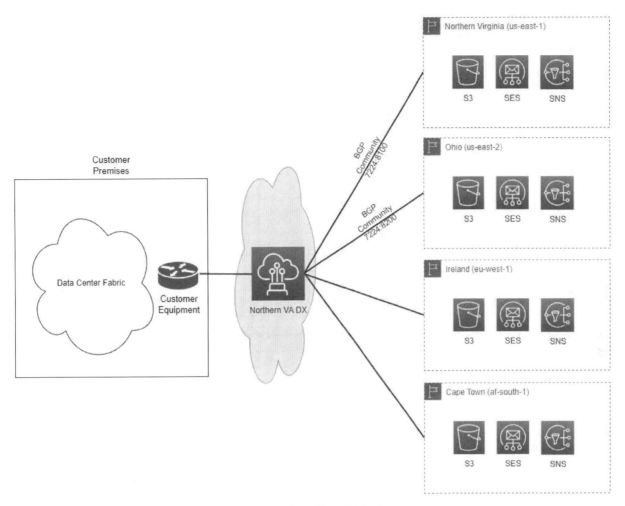

**Figure 34: Sample Public VIF Architecture**

In this example, a customer has a Public VIF on their DX that is providing connectivity to the entire AWS public zone. The diagram is a bit misleading, insofar as there are not really separate 'cables' terminating on the DX for each region, but it was important to point out that each regional advertisement is different. AWS uses several BGP communities to control route propagation and to allow network engineers to filter regional advertisements from AWS.

Based on what region the DX location is in, AWS will tag routes advertised from that region with a BGP community, and other routes advertised from the same continent with another BGP community. The rest come untagged, and this allows engineers to filter out other regions/continents out or not as requirements dictate. All routes from AWS come with the well-known NO_EXPORT BGP community tag, and it is forbidden to advertise AWS prefixes from your organization.

The goal of advertising the AWS public zone prefixes over the DX to the on-prem location is to provide more specific routing for AWS public services. Rather than using a default route to the Internet, traffic to AWS public services will use the DX instead. The use case for this depends on what public-facing resources (through public IP assignment or NAT) are intended to be able to reach AWS public services over the more reliable DX. Remember that a DX comes with direct access to the AWS backbone (or close to it, with a provider/partner) and more importantly, it comes with an SLA. There are many public zone services that might need that level of performance and protection to accomplish business objectives.

When advertising on-prem public routes to AWS over the Public VIF, BGP communities are used to control how far these prefixes can go. Any prefixes advertised to AWS over a Public VIF will only be used within the AWS network, not readvertised to the Internet or other AWS customers. The BGP community tag only determines if the routes will leave the region, continent, or be advertised throughout all AWS regions everywhere.

## AWS DX – Transit VIF

The name of this VIF probably gives away its purpose, but please act surprised anyway. The Transit VIF is a special VIF created solely to connect a DX to a Transit Gateway. This allows you to leverage the routing capabilities of a single TGW. There can be only a single Transit VIF per DX, but we'll be covering a way to split out the DX to further peer with more TGWs in a bit. The Transit VIF is not restricted to the concept of a Public or Private zone, instead, the Transit VIF works like a TGW attachment to allow the TGW to make all the decisions on connecting things together.

Here's a basic Transit VIF Architecture:

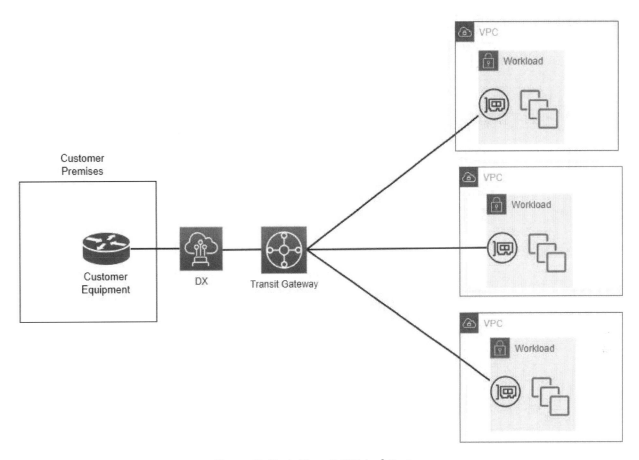

**Figure 35: Basic Transit VIF Architecture**

Why do we need this? Why couldn't this simply be a DX with three Private VIFs connected to a VGW in each VPC? It's a good question. Let's take another look at the DX architecture using network gear and it may make more sense. Here is a standard DX with a Private VIF terminating to a VGW on a VPC, no Transit Gateway:

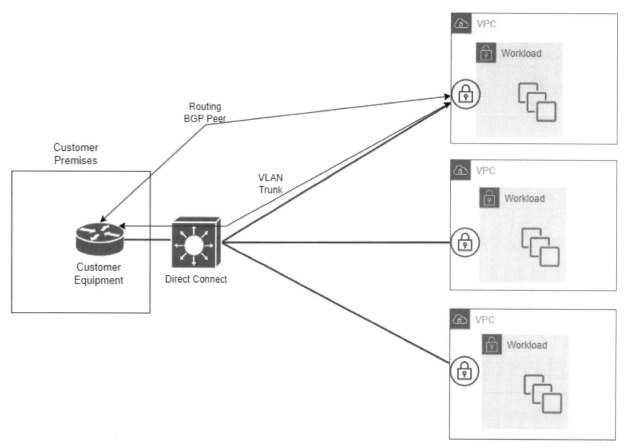

**Figure 36: Private VIF DX Architecture Using Network Icons**

Notice that the actual Layer 3 routing is happening between the on-prem device and each individual VGW attached to the VPC using a Private VIF. No BGP peering is set up with the DX itself, the peering is just using the DX like a switch. This means that the on-prem device will act as a router on a stick if BGP is not filtered. For two VPCs to communicate (outside of native peering or NVA), the traffic between them would have to come all the way out of the cloud and be routed through the on-prem equipment to reach the other VPC. If the goal is to provide connectivity within the cloud as well as to and from the cloud, this design is terrible. Not only is it inefficient, but you will also pay for the egress charges leaving the cloud even when the destination is back into the cloud.

There is also the matter of CSP limitations on how many VIFs can be created on a single DX. Each DX can only support 1 Transit VIF (as of this writing, always check the links in the appendix), but that is all that's needed given the TGW ability to route traffic within the cloud. From a cost perspective, a TGW is not free and there should be a cost comparison when building the cloud environment. Very small cloud deployments may end up overpaying for a Transit VIF with TGW for functionality they don't yet need.

Having pointed these design considerations out, let's look at this same architecture with a Transit VIF instead of Private VIFs:

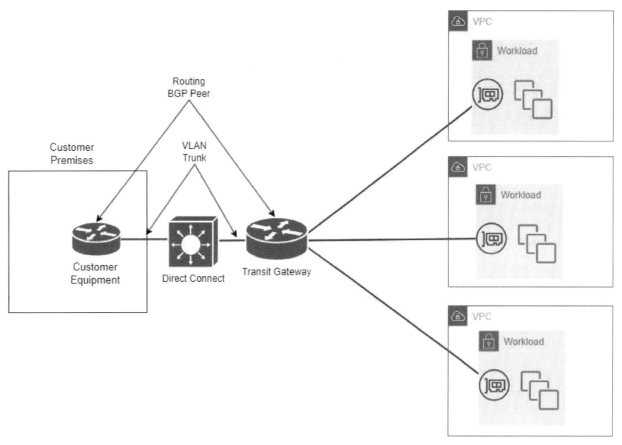

**Figure 37: Transit VIF DX Architecture Using Network Icons**

Network engineers should be able to see the value immediately. For the enterprises that need it, a Transit VIF can provide an entirely in-cloud routing experience, routed dynamically and intelligently by a TGW. Even though the Transit VIF is limited,don't forget that TGWs themselves can peer to extend the routing domain. You can also have multiple Direct Connects with their own Transit VIFs, private VIFs, and Public VIFs. This, of course, needs to be well-planned, and if the on-prem locations are cross-connected via some sort of WAN, dark fiber or other routing, the possibility exists for route loops. An entire book could be (maybe will be?) written about how to deal with those sorts of designs, but for now the important thing to understand is that the risk exists.

## AWS DX Gateway – For Private or Transit VIF Only!

The limitations on how many VIFs we can have and how we can attach them caused a lot of suboptimal routing designs. AWS introduced the DX Gateway to combat this. Before we get into DX Gateway, a quick terminology recap:

*Transit Gateway*: AWS Managed Router platform that allows static and dynamic routing between resources

*DX*: AWS Direct Connect, the private circuit that works like a Layer 2 VLAN trunk

*VIF*: Virtual Interface, a very cloudy way of saying VLAN

*VGW*: Virtual Private Gateway, a Layer 3 construct serving as a VPN/Layer 3 termination point

*VPC*: Virtual Private Cloud, a routing domain based on a CIDR supernet, segmented from other VPCs

*Private VIF*: VIF that allows access to private AWS environments like VPC via VGW peering

*Public VIF*: VIF that allows connection to public (and only public) AWS resources

*Transit VIF*: VIF to connect to a TGW, limited resource per DX

A recap was needed because the DX Gateway straddles a lot of topics with a lot of acronyms, and while we have discussed all of them, it's important to keep it fresh in mind when getting into a discussion about what is and is not possible with DX Gateway.

DX Gateway can be thought of as a virtual switch. Though we haven't focused on it very much when talking about DX, remember that DX is region-locked and has a limit of how many VIFs can be created. The DX Gateway allows us to exceed some of these limitations. The DX Gateway can only be used with Private VIFs, and to a smaller (but important) extent with Transit VIFs. The primary purpose of DX Gateway is to get around the DX region lock limitations and extend the number of VPCs that can be connected to a DX outside of a Transit VIF. Consider the following diagram:

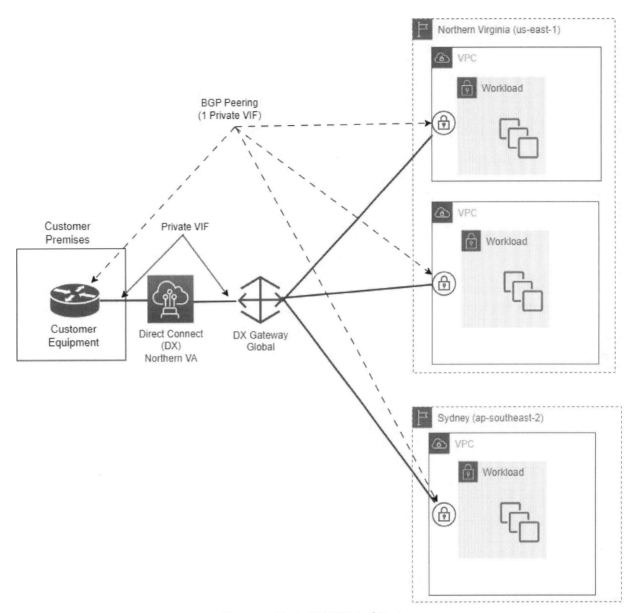

**Figure 38: Basic DX GW Architecture**

There are several important differences between this diagram and the previous ones:

• The VPCs we are connecting are in different AWS regions

• There is only one Private VIF consumed on the DX to associate with the DX Gateway

• The DX Gateway acts like a switch, passing through connectivity to VGWs

• The customer equipment will have three different BGP peers on one Private VIF

While the diagram may appear similar to the one we examined when discussing Transit VIFs, the DX Gateway has no routing intelligence, and traffic must traverse the customer equipment to go between VPCs. The DX Gateway is solely a global AWS construct to allow the DX connections to scale out to other regions and scale up in terms of total VPC attachments.

As always, check the appendix for links to the most up-to-date information, but the DX Gateway can use a single Private VIF on the DX to connect to (as of now) 10 different VPCs, instead of a one-to-one relationship using just the DX itself.

Just as importantly, the DX Gateway allows a DX in any region to connect VPCs in other regions, though it is worth noting that this will come with data transfer charges. The DX Gateway itself does not cost anything, unlike TGW, but transferring data between AWS regions will.

Speaking of TGW, the DX Gateway also extends the abilities of a DX to interact with TGWs using its single Transit VIF. You can create multiple DX Gateways, but there is a limitation on what can be connected. Specifically, a DX Gateway can do Private VIFs or Transit VIFs, but not both together. Let's examine an extension of the previous diagram and add a second DX Gateway for a Transit VIF. Here's how it works:

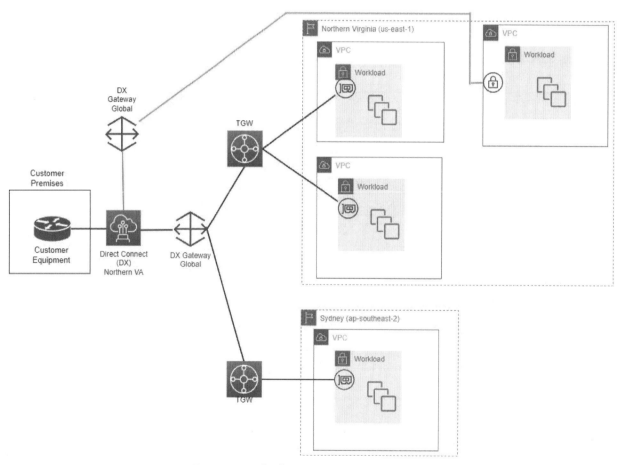

**Figure 39: Multiple DX Gateway Architecture**

There can be multiple DX Gateways, as each one must be dedicated to service either Private or Transit VIFs. In this example, we migrated most of the workloads to TGW while keeping one on a Private VIF. In the real world, requirements for traffic dictate these sorts of decisions. This is just illustrative.

Pay attention to some implied requirements and limitations:

• We need multiple TGWs because TGW is a region-specific construct.

• The TGWs are NOT peered together. This means that as of right now in this diagram, the TGWs must traverse the DX and customer equipment to communicate. The better design, if cross-region communication is needed, would be to peer the TGWs.

• Remember that while DX Gateway is global, it has no route intelligence. It is basically a virtual switch allowing more connections on DX-based VIFs.

• We need multiple DX Gateways as we are using a combination of Private and Transit VIFs

Let's focus on what this setup looks like from a network perspective, and it might make more sense. Remember that though we are using switches to explain, there are no spanning-tree concerns or Layer 2 limitations worth considering here:

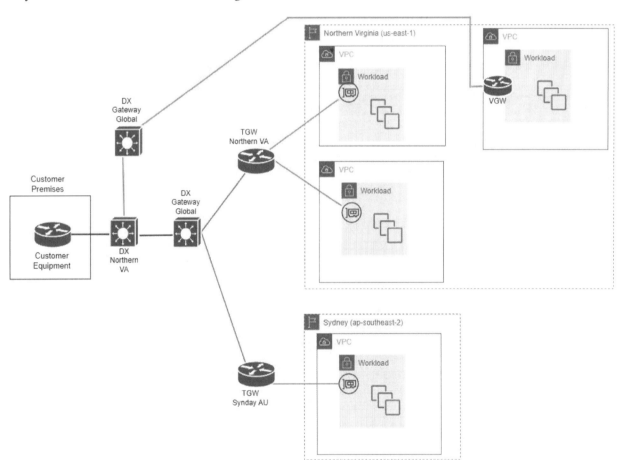

Figure 40:Multiple DX Gateways with Network Icons

The DX Gateway attached to the TGWs is acting like a switch connecting the two TGWs to the on-prem customer equipment, but the two TGWs cannot communicate using the DX Gateway. If a packet were to traverse from the workload attached to the Northern Virginia TGW, it would have to go all the way back to the customer premises equipment,which might or might not forward that to the Sydney TGW (through the DX gateway) based on how BGP routing is configured.

DX Gateways extend the reach of a DX to peer with TGWs by allowing a single Transit VIF to peer with multiple TGWs. The TGWs themselves can also connect to each other through TGW peering. Lastly, the TGWs can be connected to multiple DX Gateways, and this makes things capable of spinning out of control very quickly if proper network design isn't followed. One last diagram, to give an idea of how quickly the design can spiral out of control without due diligence and planning:

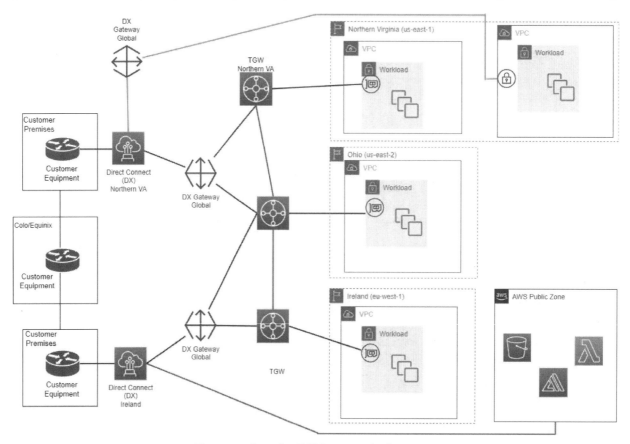

**Figure 41: Complex DX Gateway Architecture**

Now imagine having to do Route Table manipulation in the cloud, on all of the VPCs and TGWs, route filtering on the on-prem side to prevent routing loops, and extra connections for redundancy (a few were included here to start the brain panicking), and you can see how quickly cloud networking can become extremely complicated. Your mission is to design better networks than this.

# Network Virtual Appliances

By now we are familiar with the concept that NVAs are like networking cheat codes for the cloud. It's not exactly correct, of course, as all NVAs are constrained by the underlying cloud constructs, but there is something about being able to deploy a network-focused platform with all the granularity and control that engineers are used to using. The good news is when it comes to extracloud connectivity, the NVAs shine just as brightly. It's almost trivial to explain how an NVA works compared to the complexity of native cloud architectures, but for completeness it is important to discuss some of the ways an NVA can be leveraged to connect things like a VPN or DX.

A DX can't terminate directly on an NVA, but it is possible to connect using a DX in a manner that uses the underlying cloud Route Tables and constructs only as an underlay, building an IPsec or GRE tunnel over it. This allows you to avoid things like route limitations, and because both ends of the connection are true network appliances, it's possible to use any routing protocol that is supported. Let's look at how this might work in a few diagrams:

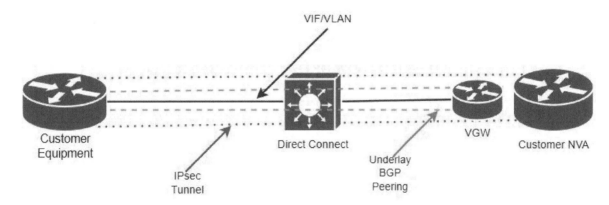

**Figure 42: Tunnel Between Routers Using DX Underlay**

Let's look at it now using the cloud constructs.

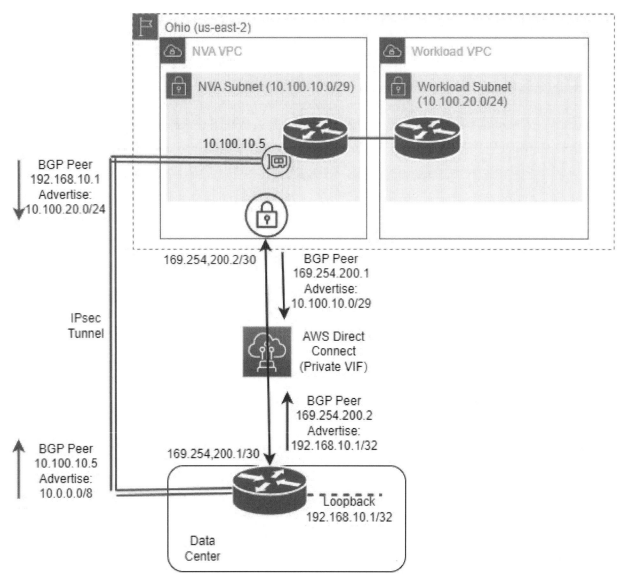

**Figure 43: Overlay/Underlay NVA DX Architecture**

Okay, there's a lot going on here, so let's break it down.

First, there is the DX. The DX works the same as it did in prior explanations. There is a VIF, in this case, a Private VIF, connecting on-prem equipment to a VGW that's attached to a VPC in which we have an NVA. Let's assume it's a router in this case, but any appliance that can terminate an IPsec tunnel and peer with BGP would do.

Over that connection, the on-prem equipment will usually have an underlay VRF solely for the purpose of creating an IPsec tunnel. It will peer with the VGW across the DX and advertise some prefix to use as the IPsec endpoint to the VGW, which needs to be configured to program that prefix into the VPC Route Table.

Meanwhile, the VGW will advertise the CIDR of the NVA VPC to the on-prem equipment using BGP. Now, both sides are aware of how to reach the endpoint IP addresses of the other side to create an IPsec tunnel overlay. The two devices build that IPsec tunnel,and then peer BGP over that tunnel.

What's important to understand now is that the cloud native constructs are blissfully unaware of the prefixes being exchanged across that tunnel, so there are no concerns about limitations on number of prefixes (other than the device's own limitations). The NVA will usually be connected to other VPCs as was explained earlier in this book,and the prefix exchange happens right over the top of the cloud.

Lastly, at some point we absolutely must bring cloud native Route Tables back into the picture. While the NVA VPC will not have any workloads, the connected VPCs will.

Those VPCs have the cloud native VPC router, and that router needs to know what destinations lead to other parts of the network. Commonly, a supernet route is added to direct traffic to the Elastic Network Interface (ENI) of the NVA since it will have the routing intelligence and connectivity.

The entire reason of using NVAs in place of cloud native is to have an elevated level of control, visibility, and features. However, NVAs can make things more complicated as well, so care must be taken to use them where they make sense. For example, while adding an NVA gives you the controls of the appliance's operating system, it also adds a layer of complexity in that there are at least two Route Tables to account for,and neither are aware of the other: the NVA and the native. We can design hybrid infrastructures that blend some or all the things together, either by using a series of NVAs to stretch a fabric and localizing cloud native routing to workload subnets, or we can integrate with more intelligent native routing constructs like AWS TGW.

Here is a sample NVA/TGW design:

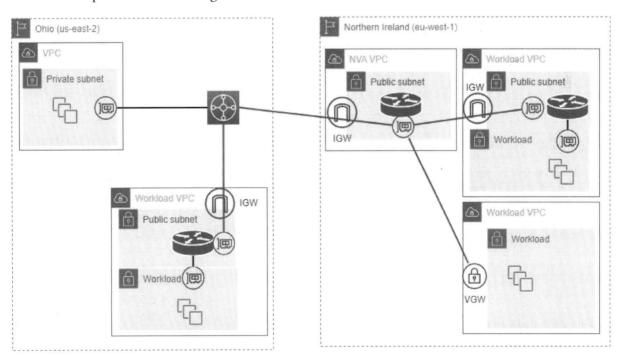

**Figure 44: Illustrative NVA and Native Cloud Architecture**

In the above diagram, the red lines indicate IPsec tunnels built over public IP addresses, and the black line is a simple TGW attachment. We covered how both options work earlier in the book. The TGW also supports attachment via IPsec tunnel from an NVA or on-prem equipment. NVAs can connect to a VGW in the same way on-prem equipment can, working as a CGW in that case. Hybrid cloud networking offers a lot of options, the key is to understand the strengths and limitations of each, which we have been discussing throughout the book.

This design is not any sort of best practice or recommendation, it is simply to show some of the many possibilities. Remember, this book is not intended to provide best practices and design recommendations, the goal has been and continues to be arming network engineers with the terminology and understanding of what options are available. Design follows requirements and knowing your options will arm you best to deliver business outcomes. It is possible in the future that a book focused on design could be forthcoming, but before one can design anything, they need to understand what's in the toolbox.

NVAs are an easy way to connect AWS to other resources, within the same region, between regions, between different clouds, or between on-prem and the cloud. NVAs are the most familiar and understandable of the options, but the underlying cloud routing cannot be completely ignored. Also, depending on the design, NVAs could be more costly than a native option that does not require the same level of route intelligence. Always keep an eye on the cost of the solution and weigh it against what value is added, or what complexity is taken away.

# Client VPN

Perhaps the least impressive or interesting extracloud connectivity option is the AWS Client VPN. It's a very bare-bones implementation of what we would refer to as an SSL VPN (even though it uses TLS now). It's included here for completeness, but it is a solution that is very basic.

It utilizes OpenVPN as the client endpoint software, and the actual VPN headend service is configured in AWS and attached to a VPC. That VPC should have dedicated IP space for VPN clients to use when they connect to access cloud resources. If the resources are elsewhere, such as within other VPCs, some form of connectivity and routing must exist for the VPN clients to be able to access those resources. Here's the basic configuration of the AWS Client VPN. As you will see, it's extremely basic.

Client IPv4 CIDR  Info
The IP address range, in CIDR notation, from which client IP addresses are allocated.

Q   10.0.0.0/22

CIDR block cannot be larger than /12 or smaller than /22.

## Authentication information  Info

Server certificate ARN
The server certificate must be provisioned with or imported into AWS Certificate Manager (ACM).

Select certificate                                                        ▼

Authentication options
Choose one or a combination of authentication methods to use.

☐  Use mutual authentication

☑  Use user-based authentication

User-based authentication options

◉  Active directory authentication

◯  Federated authentication

Directory ID
The ID of the AWS directory services directory to use.

Select directory ID                                                       ▼

## Connection logging  Info

◖  Enable log details on client connections
    Use connection logs to have forensics on when clients attempted to connect.

## Client connect handler  Info

◖  Enable client connect handler

The authentication options are either certificate or user based. Certificate-based authentication is very well known and will not be further explained. If authentication based on a user, the authentication store can be an AWS directory ID or a federated SAML provider. The client logging simply logs connection attempts, but the client handler is an interesting option. Think of something like Cisco ISE or ClearPass that can identify and authorize users based on attributes. AWS offers the ability to do something similar, but only through AWS Lambda, which means that a client connection would invoke an AWS Lambda serverless function that would need to profile the user and return some sort of yes/no decision to the AWS VPN authentication service.

Beyond that, the AWS VPN has all the comforts of a normal VPN service:

## Other parameters - *optional*

**DNS server 1 IP address**
The IP address of the DNS server to use. There are no default DNS servers.

> 10.0.0.0

**DNS server 2 IP address**
The IP address of the DNS server to use. There are no default DNS servers.

> 10.0.0.1

**Transport protocol**   Info
Transport protocol used by the TLS sessions.

◉ UDP

◯ TCP

🔘 **Enable split-tunnel**   Info

**VPC ID**

> vpc-0140149df3f335532                                                    ▼

**Security group IDs**
Security groups to be applied to the endpoint.

> Select security groups                                                    ▼

> sg-0b8a26fc7a84c1b38 (default)  ✕
> default VPC security group

**VPN port**
AWS client VPN supports ports 443 and 1194 for both TCP and UDP.

> 443                                                                       ▼

🔘 **Enable self-service portal**   Info

**Session timeout hours**   Info

> 24                                                                        ▼

🔘 **Enable client login banner**   Info

The VPN client can receive special DNS servers if needed to resolve cloud-based private resources. Split-tunneling can be enabled or disabled for users, so that non-AWS traffic will go from the client locally instead of through the VPN. The VPC to which clients will be placed on connection must be selected, along with a Security Group (discussed in detail later) to apply to the VPN clients. This will act as a VPN User firewall. The next section will be on AWS network security, and we will discuss SG more in that section.

If the self-service web portal is needed, it can be activated to allow remote VPN clients to download OpenVPN and the VPN configuration. That's about all there is to say for AWS Client VPN. It's very basic, there are many limitations (see appendix), and it is charged on an hourly basis.

We didn't cover this in the section on NVA extracloud connectivity, but it is also possible to use an NVA for remote access VPN in the same way that you would do so in an on-prem data center. The NVA simply needs to be accessible from the Internet and offer remote access service. Most firewalls can be configured to act as remote access VPNs, as well as some router NVAs. The main requirement with using an NVA is ensuring that the ENI that clients will use for VPN tunneling is accessible from the outside and allows the connection. Of course, you still need to deal with the standard configuration of the NVA itself. The VPN clients need to be authenticated and the NVA needs to be able to reach the auth store on the correct ports. The cloud does not obviate the need for basic networking, nor does it offer magic solutions to common problems after all.

# Securing AWS Networks

Network security goes hand in hand with network engineering, whether we manage it ourselves or have an infosec team that dictates the security policy. AWS offers us some very impressive network security options, from the VM level all the way to the whole cloud network. Let's work our way out from the simplest to most complex options.

## Security Groups

We don't really have an analog for Security Groups in the network world. The closest thing to compare them to would be ACLs that can be applied to the NIC of a virtual appliance. The reality is slightly different and there are VM host-based ACLs in the middle of the stack, but part of the benefit of running all the infrastructure as an SDN fabric is the ability to provide security in places that were impossible before. Here is what it looks like to create a Security Group. Notice that the SG includes both ingress and egress rules:

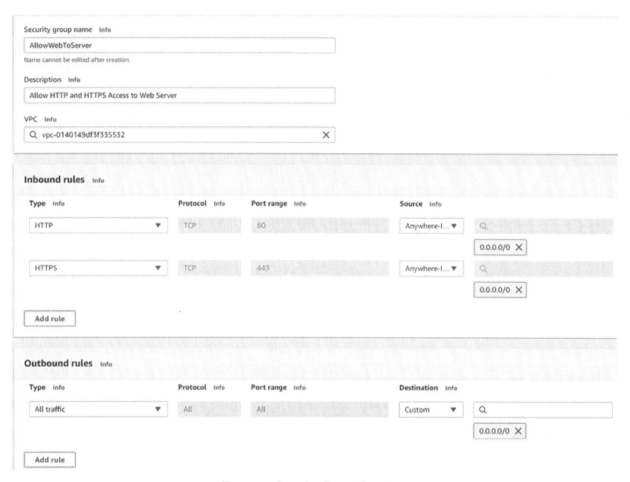

**Figure 45: Security Group Creation**

Look familiar? Yes, it's just a fancy access list. The difference is that this ACL applies to an ENI or service (which usually has an abstracted ENI anyway). This allows granular ACLs to apply at the interface level. The normal way to use SGs is to only allow what's needed on ingress and allow anything to egress from the ENI. This scales better than individually managing what each ENI has access to on egress, and besides, SGs can only allow traffic, not deny it. The deny is implicit and cannot be specifically configured. Importantly, an SG is a stateful construct. This means that we do not require rules to be created to allow traffic to both ingress and egress. The SG keeps track of the connection.

Security Groups do have a maximum number of lines, and as always, the most up to date details of limitations and numbers will be in the appendix. SGs can be applied broadly or granularly, and wherever they are applied the same rules take effect. As an example, like VMs could share SGs like this:

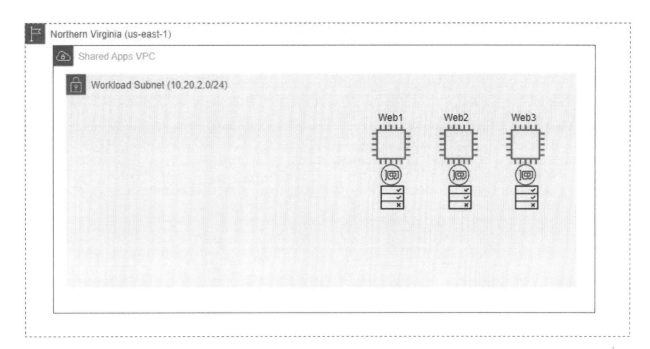

Create a single SG, apply it to as many ENIs as needed, and the rules will be enforced across all the VMs. Because the SG is enforced at the ENI level, we can also use it to enforce microsegmentation within the same subnet in a way that normally would require VLAN segmentation through a security appliance to enforce.

Consider the following:

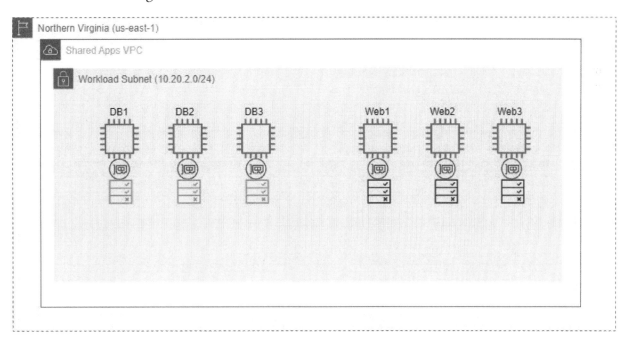

The normal approach to network security would be to segment these servers into different VLANs, subnets and possibly force the routing to take the traffic between them through a firewall. Security

Groups can enforce at the NIC level, so there is no need for complex network security so long as the SG supports the rules needed.

It should be noted that SGs do not do deep packet inspection and operate at Layer 4.

You can specify protocols, ports, and IP addresses to allow. Interestingly, you can also specify other SGs to allow as well. This is helpful if you have a fleet of servers that should be able to communicate but don't want to manage SGs every time a new server is built, or in the case of cloud elasticity when Auto Scaling Groups kick in and create more VMs in respond to demand.

Let's assume we create an SG called AllowWebToServer that allows web clients to reach the server website, but we also want to allow (only) other web servers to communicate on the backend using port 8080. With an ACL this would be almost impossible to do automatically. When a new server is created, with a new ENI, the SG would have to be updated with a new Allow rule for the host IP of the new server.

Instead, what we do is add a rule that allows the traffic from any ENI with a certain SG attached, and no host routes or subnets are needed. A new web server built by automation will automatically receive that SG attached to its NIC/ENI and it will be allowed to communicate with the other web servers. Here is how this is configured:

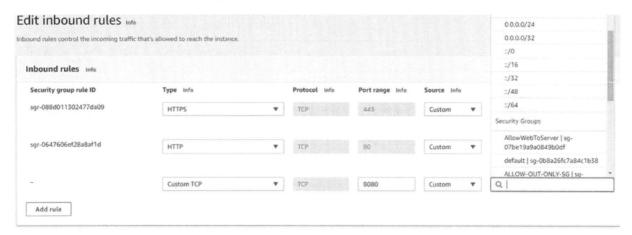

It's also common to use this in a shared services setup because it makes communication between applications very simple. In the above example, showing Web and DB servers in the same subnet, the servers could be configured with an SG based on what should be able to access them and simply reference the SG attached to the other set of servers for cross-server communication.

As network engineers, this server-level example may seem out of our wheelhouse, but it will absolutely impact traffic and so it needs to be understood. One thing to bring this back to the network side, as an example, would be a security appliance.

Imagine a firewall with multiple ENIs attached as seen several times through this book. The SG attached to those ENIs could severely complicate the troubleshooting process if the SG is not allowing certain traffic to reach the firewall itself. The common best practice for security appliances is to open the SG wide for the data plane ENIs and use SG lockdown on the management interface.

This way, the configuration, enforcement, and troubleshooting can take place entirely on the firewall itself. We'll discuss this briefly in a dedicated section on NVAs.

If Security Groups offer such a granular level of control, why even move on? Surely the SG is the only security construct required? We can't stop at SGs for many reasons,not least of which is the SG construct has a limited number of rules. Let's move up and out and talk about the next layer of security, and one which will be the most familiar: Network ACLs.

# Network ACLs

Hopefully, we won't need to spend a lot of time reviewing how a network ACL works. Instead, let's focus on how NACLs are applied in AWS and how they differ from the ones you apply to traditional network devices. First, a refresher:

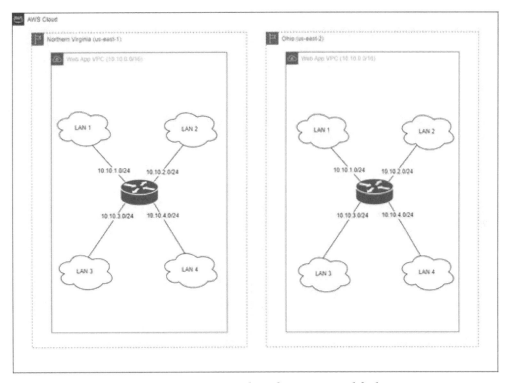

**Figure 4: VPC Network Architecture Simplified**

Subnets are a logical carving of a VPC supernet into smaller networks. Each subnet is tied to an AWS Availability Zone. It's common but not required to locate different subnets in different AZ for redundancy. While the VPC Router isn't an actual appliance, it does use constructs like Subnets and Route Tables to decide how to forward traffic.

Network ACLs can be applied to subnets. Each subnet can have exactly one NACL applied,but the NACL can be applied to multiple subnets. Subnets are tied to VPCs, and so are NACLs, and this means that a NACL cannot be moved from one VPC to another. It also means that NACLs must be created for each VPC that needs one. Let's look at the previous example, but with NACLs in place:

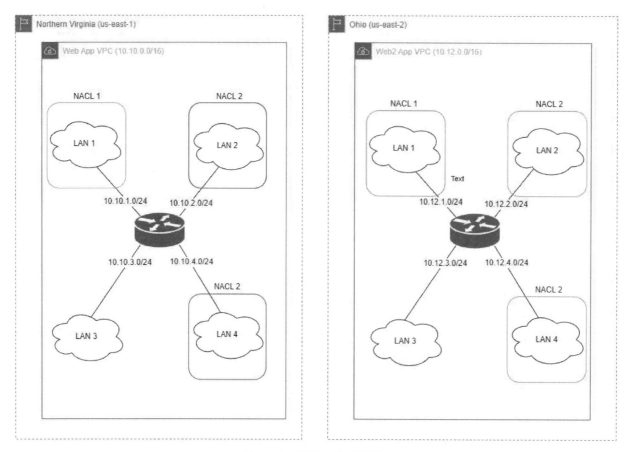

**Figure 46: VPC with NACLs**

In the above diagram, we have a subnet with an NACL, two subnets sharing a different NACL, and another subnet with no NACL at all. The two VPCs have NACLs with the same name, but they are different VPCs entirely, and so the NACLs are different as well. Here is what the NACL looks like configured:

**Inbound rules** (4)

Q *Filter inbound rules*

| Rule number ▽ | Type ▽ | Protocol ▽ | Port range ▽ | Source ▽ | Allow/Deny |
|---|---|---|---|---|---|
| 10 | All ICMP - IPv4 | ICMP (1) | All | 0.0.0.0/0 | ⊘ Allow |
| 12 | SSH (22) | TCP (6) | 22 | 10.0.0.0/8 | ⊘ Allow |
| 13 | All traffic | All | All | 0.0.0.0/0 | ⊗ Deny |

Let's tackle it in pieces. First comes the rule number. Just as with network ACLs on network devices, the ACL sequence is evaluated from the top down. This means the correct behavior is to put the most specific rules near the top, where the top is the lowest number. The Type/Protocol/Port section refers to the kind of traffic, its port,protocol, application, etc. There also exists the choice for all IPv4 traffic, all IPv6 traffic, or both. This is almost exactly like a network ACL on routers, and the only part worth adding is to recall if the traffic is being allowed inbound or outbound so the appropriate ports can be selected.

The Source field refers to the IP range of the traffic. Note that this picture is of an inbound NACL rule. The outbound rule refers to a Destination instead, but in both cases, it refers to a CIDR range from 0 to 32 (a host route). Lastly, we either allow or deny the traffic. This is not groundbreaking, but like all things in the cloud, NACLs have a limited number of rules and there are a limited number of NACLs that can be created. Let's cover the other things that are important when thinking about NACLs in the cloud:

• NACLs are **stateless**. This is very important. Because state is not tracked, an NACL requires matching rules for inbound and outbound to allow traffic. This is different than the SGs which are stateful.

• NACLs will either be consulted before or after SGs, depending on the direction of traffic flow. If traffic is coming to a virtual machine from outside the subnet, the traffic will hit the NACL first before reaching the SG. If traffic is leaving the VM, the SG will be used first, and if traffic leaves the subnet, the NACL will be consulted.

• NACLs are useless if all traffic stays within the same subnet. Only traffic crossing a subnet boundary is subject to NACL, this is the same behavior as a router with an ACL on its interface. If traffic does not come through the interface, the ACL is not used.

Let's visualize the SG and NACL together and it should make sense:

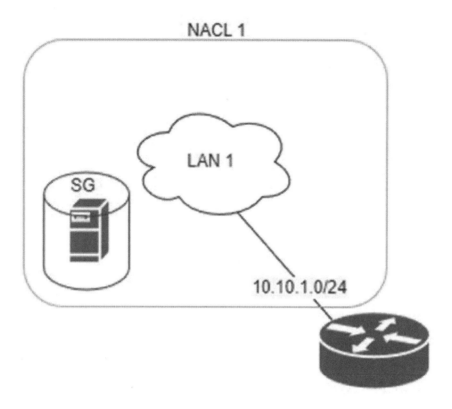

If traffic is leaving the VM, it must hit the SG first. If traffic is coming to the VM from outside the subnet, it must hit the NACL first. If traffic stays within the subnet, no NACL is used, only SG. Remember this when planning network security deployments and when troubleshooting.

## AWS Network Firewall

Way back at the start of the book, we discussed the possibility of manipulating Route Tables and using ENIs attached to a firewall appliance to redirect traffic to a firewall. In that example, we were discussing situations where you might need different RTs per subnet, but if we take the firewall NVA out of the picture, that is what AWS Network Firewall is doing. AWS is managing a firewall appliance and exposing an endpoint to be placed within VPC subnets, where needed, and RTs must be manipulated to redirect traffic to that endpoint. Traffic will hit the endpoint, tunnel to the AWS managed firewall, be inspected, and if allowed, returned to the VPC to continue.

A single-VPC Internet egress-focused AWS Firewall architecture looks like this:

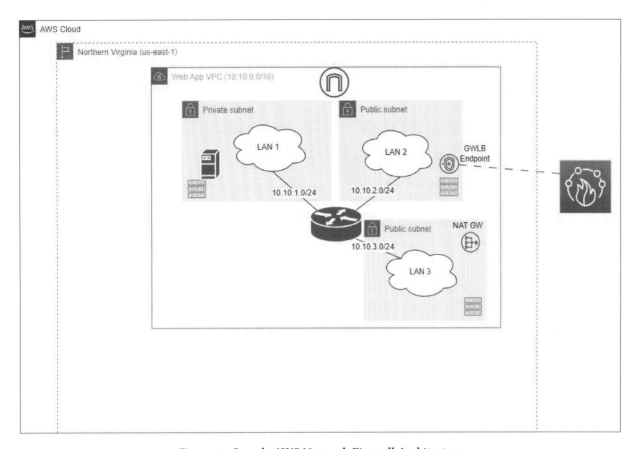

**Figure 47: Sample AWS Network Firewall Architecture**

The AWS Firewall is used to inspect traffic within and between VPCs, depending on the use cases. This goes back to what we discussed about manipulating RTs and using ENIs to do things like service insertion for security. As we talk more about the complex network services AWS provides, we'll need to start pulling these different concepts together into a whole. Remember that each subnet can have a custom Route Table, and that the VPC Router will use that custom RT when making decisions about where to send traffic from that subnet.

Creating an AWS Firewall in a VPC requires specifying what subnets will be protected by the firewall, and what subnet the firewall should place an Endpoint ENI. We discussed endpoints and ENIs earlier, so the concept should be familiar. What we have not yet discussed is the Gateway Load Balancer behind the endpoint. Load balancers are next, but for now, imagine that the GWLB creates redundancy on the firewall stack by load balancing inspection traffic to more than one firewall, pinning the sessions to the correct one. AWS manages the fleet of firewalls in this case so you don't have to, like how you might use a managed firewall service with an MSP.

In this case, referring to Figure 48 above, let's discuss a traffic flow to the Internet from the server in the private subnet to the Internet and back:

1. Traffic leaves the VM in LAN1 private subnet. The RT has been modified so that traffic to 0.0.0.0/0 goes to the NAT Gateway in LAN3.

2. The NAT Gateway performs a NAT on the private traffic using its own address. The subnet RT of the LAN3 subnet directs traffic to 0.0.0.0/0 to the ENI of the GWLB endpoint (firewall interface) for inspection.

3. Traffic hits the endpoint and is tunneled to a fleet of AWS managed firewall instances elsewhere. The firewall rules that you define when creating the AWS firewall are consulted. If traffic is allowed, it is returned to the public subnet in the VPC.

4. The RT in LAN2 is consulted, and the next hop of 0.0.0.0/0 is the Internet Gateway. Importantly, the AWS Firewall does NOT perform NAT on the traffic.

5. The IGW uses the NAT Gateway Elastic IP 1:1 NAT and sends traffic to the Internet.

6. On return, traffic goes from the IGW to the ENI of the GWLB Endpoint via VPC Ingress Routing/Edge Association (discussed in the IGW section, this is modifying the IGW RT to point to the GWLB endpoint instead of the VPC Router IP).

7. The traffic is again tunneled, inspected, returned, and sent back to the NAT Gateway to have the NAT removed.

8. The NAT GW reverses the NAT, consults the LAN3 RT, and sends the traffic back to the private workload.

That was a lot. Try to take it a step at a time, referring to the diagram in Figure 45, but also referring to the other parts of the book that cover these moving pieces.

The constructs doing the heavy lifting here are the different RTs. We can almost think of them as different VRFs in the way they are being used. If this were an on-prem type of deployment, redirecting traffic through a firewall often requires inside and outside VLANs connected to route and switch infrastructure. We have no VLANs in the cloud (that we can access), but we do have the ability to redirect traffic in a similar way with route tables, and that is what was done here.

We can also use the AWS firewall to protect inter-VPC traffic the same way. Imagine that instead of redirecting to an IGW, we redirected traffic to a VPC peering or a Transit Gateway. We could drop that NAT Gateway so long as the VPC CIDRs did not overlap and make it a lot simpler. The common deployment using Transit Gateway looks something like a centralized Firewall inspection model we see on-prem. In that case, the RT manipulation needed to redirect traffic through the firewalls is based on the TGW attachments.

Here's a diagram to make it easier to understand:

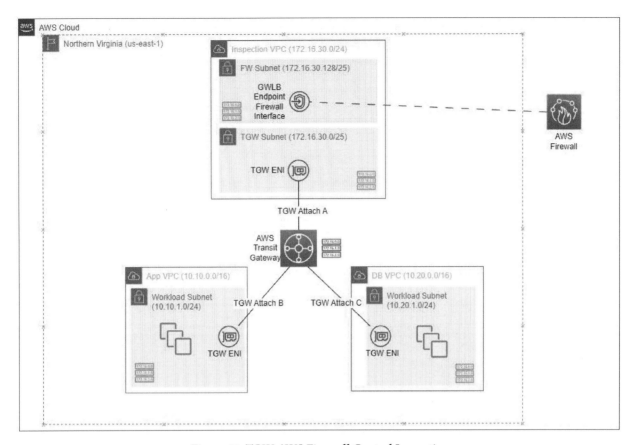

**Figure 48: TGW AWS Firewall Central Inspection**

This is a different use case, using AWS Firewall to do inter-VPC inspection. To be clear, AWS Firewall could do both, we could add an egress strategy to that VPC, or we could add an Egress VPC attached to TGW and manipulate the routing like we would with VRFs and VLANs on-prem. Rather than get too complex, though, let's talk through the traffic flow of a central firewall inspection zone using Transit Gateway just using an inter-VPC example.

Here's what the TGW attachments look like from an RT perspective. You may recognize this diagram from the section on TGW, it's just been modified:

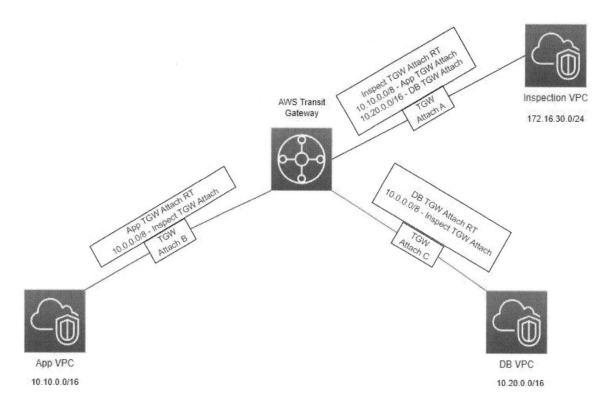

**Figure 49: Central Firewall TGW Attachment RTs**

Figure 48 and Figure 49 should help explain the traffic flow as we step through it below:

1. Packet leaves VM in App VPC workload subnet with a destination of 10.20.1.50, a workload in the DB VPC.
2. The RT of the subnet shows the next-hop for all traffic that isn't local should be sent the ENI of the TGW. Traffic is forwarded to the TGW attachment.
3. TGW Attachment B Route Table shows all traffic to 10.0.0.0/8 should be forwarded to the Inspection VPC attachment and down to the TGW ENI in that VPC.
4. The TGW Subnet in the Inspection VPC has a next-hop of 0.0.0.0/0 to the GWLB endpoint firewall interface in the FW subnet, so traffic is forwarded to the GWLB Endpoint in the other subnet.
5. The traffic hits the endpoint, is tunneled to the AWS Firewall, inspected, allowed or denied. If allowed, traffic comes back through the tunnel to the FW Subnet.
6. The FW subnet RT has a next-hop of 0.0.0.0/0 pointed at the TGW Attachment. Traffic is routed from the FW subnet to the TGW attachment.
7. When TGW Attachment A gets the traffic, it routes based on the attachment RT to the DB VPC.
8. Traffic is received in the DB VPC workload subnet and sent to the DB VM.
9. When the DB VM responds, the destination is now 10.10.1.50, the workload in the App VPC.
10. Without repeating all the steps, the subnet RT routes the traffic back to the TGW, TGW Attach C routes it to the Inspection VPC, and so on.

Here's a similar setup as we would see it in an on-prem world:

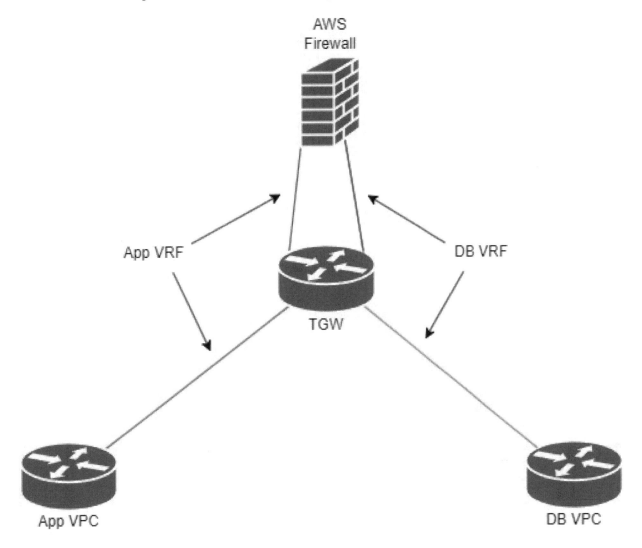

**Figure 50: Central Firewall Architecture - Traditional Network**

In this sort of setup, the firewall has either a subinterface or a dedicated interface for each VRF. The TGW in the center would place the interface to the App VPC router and the upstream firewall interface dedicated to the App VPC in the App VPC VRF, ensuring that traffic to the DB VPC would have to go through the firewall and could not just go straight through the router. That's essentially what the TGW attachment and VPC subnet manipulation does. It's a clean design and scales to many attached VPCs.

Let's move on to AWS Load Balancers. If you thought this was complex, we saved the best for last.

# Load Balancing AWS Networks

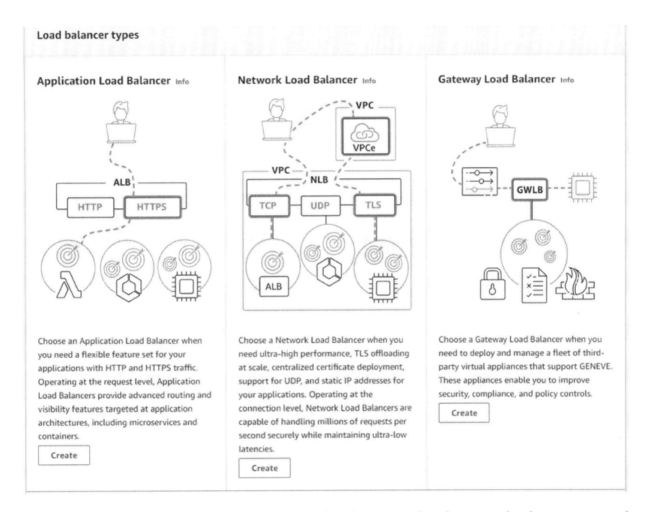

**Load balancer types**

**Application Load Balancer** Info

ALB
HTTP — HTTPS

Choose an Application Load Balancer when you need a flexible feature set for your applications with HTTP and HTTPS traffic. Operating at the request level, Application Load Balancers provide advanced routing and visibility features targeted at application architectures, including microservices and containers.

Create

**Network Load Balancer** Info

VPC
VPCe
VPC
NLB
TCP — UDP — TLS
ALB

Choose a Network Load Balancer when you need ultra-high performance, TLS offloading at scale, centralized certificate deployment, support for UDP, and static IP addresses for your applications. Operating at the connection level, Network Load Balancers are capable of handling millions of requests per second securely while maintaining ultra-low latencies.

Create

**Gateway Load Balancer** Info

GWLB

Choose a Gateway Load Balancer when you need to deploy and manage a fleet of third-party virtual appliances that support GENEVE. These appliances enable you to improve security, compliance, and policy controls.

Create

AWS offers several load balancer options for cloud applications. The Classic Load Balancer is omitted because it is no longer a recommended deployment in AWS, and the use cases are covered by these other options. Now, network engineers have always existed at or near the fringe of managing load balancers, so no assumption will be made on prior knowledge of how load balancing works.

Load balancing is simply the concept of providing a front-end destination from which the connectivity to multiple back-end resources can be managed. This can be accomplished many ways, and not all require an appliance. For example, a DNS record could contain the IP addresses of multiple servers performing the same function, so that when connecting to a specific URL or DNS name, the DNS server might return any of the server IP addresses.

This is a very simple form of load balancing, but it's also only useful for very simple use cases. What if each of three servers were serving content that required making an account, so you sign up on whichever server the DNS entry returns, but next time the DNS server gives you a different server? If the three servers in this example aren't synchronized, you might have to create an account on a totally new server. For all but the simplest of use cases, we need a way to handle connections in a more intelligent way.

The idea of a load balancer is probably well understood, but just to ensure that the networking portion of it is also well understood, let's tackle a very basic (non-AWS, generic) load balancing workflow. From there, we can split into the load balancing options AWS provides.

Let's cover load balancing in a short but sweet diagram:

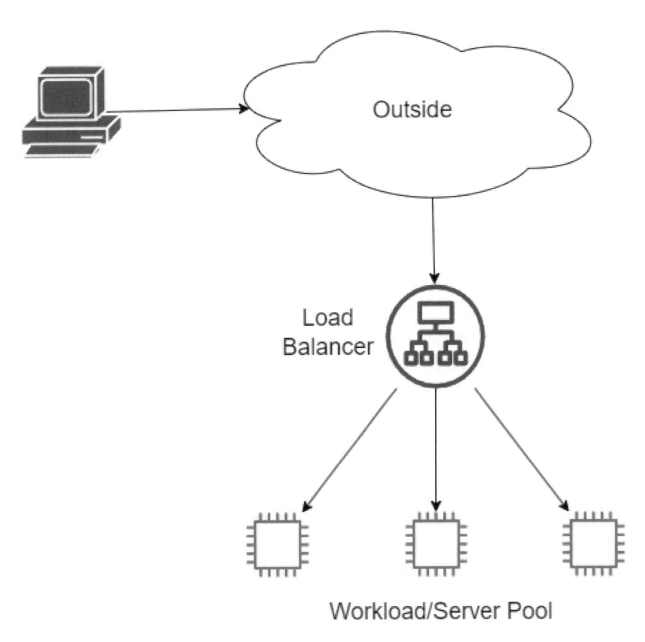

**Figure 51: Basic Load Balancing Example**

In this case, a user is connecting to the front-end IP or DNS name of an appliance set up to do load balancing. The load balancer has network connectivity to resources behind it, and any good load balancer is checking the health of those resources to ensure they are ready to receive connections.

In many ways, a Load Balancer is like a firewall. It manages front-end connectivity for resources behind the protected interfaces. It creates and tracks the state of connections through it, this is done to make sure that each connection is routed to and from the proper requestors. The load balancer may even need to perform a NAT, swapping the requestor IP for its own local IP to ensure that responses from back-end servers come back to the load balancer with the session information. This is common when using multiple load balancers for redundancy, if two load balancers are both creating back-end connections, the responding servers need to send responses back to the load balancer with session info.

Okay, let's tackle the easiest load balancer for network engineers to understand first, the NLB or Network Load Balancer.

# Network Load Balancer

This option will be the most familiar to network engineers. Honestly, the other two stretch what knowledge you are likely to have a lot more, but hopefully understanding how the NLB works will give a leg up on understanding the other ones AWS offers.

The NLB is a service construct from the AWS customer point of view. Like NAT Gateway and IGW, it is a managed service that cannot be logged into or configured outside of a few options. It is a Layer 4 load balancer, meaning it will not interpret or act based on any application-level data. It acts according to ports and protocols. The NLB must be either Internet-facing or internal. This is used to place the load balancer ENI within the appropriate subnet in a VPC and governs whether they will have an Elastic IP in addition to a private IP in the subnet. The NLB CAN be issued a static IP which helps it to be allowed through security stacks much more easily when it comes to things like hybrid networking. The NLB also works with PrivateLink technology, if internal. Here is an Internet-facing NLB architecture:

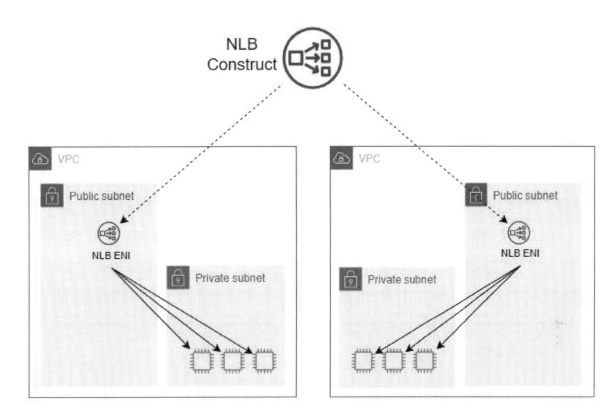

**Figure 52: Sample Internet-Facing NLB Architecture**

Importantly, these NLB interfaces are highly available and self-healing. If the interface fails for some reason, AWS will replace it. However, as a subnet-specific interface, it is only AZ-redundant, not region-redundant. For that reason, it's common to duplicate NLB interfaces and application stacks to other VPCs or subnets.

Each NLB interface must be configured with a target group, which is the list of back-end servers or services to which it will send incoming requests.

The NLB also must be configured with a listener. The listener is a service that is open and waiting for connections. The listener will, well.. listen, based on the port and protocol incoming to the NLB and set up a connection to the target back-end group,tracking its state and session. Multiple listeners can be configured for an NLB, which means that a single NLB could provide load balancer services for multiple Layer 4 applications. You could have an NLB listen for TCP/UDP 53 traffic and have a target group of DNS servers at the same time as RADIUS or some other application. The only limitation is the number of connections. Because the NLB is Layer 4 and not application-layer, its performance is vastly improved over the Application Load Balancer and can scale into the millions, so this is generally not a concern.

Let's look at one more NLB architecture and then we will move on to Application Load Balancing.

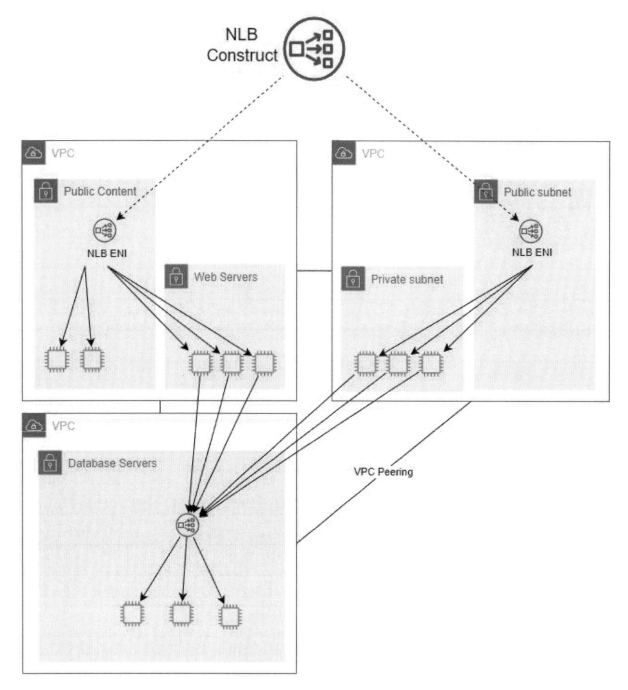

**Figure 53: Multi-tier NLB Architecture**

Internet-facing NLBs can service public and private workloads. In this example, a different listener is set up for some public-facing application running on a few public servers, and the NLB also services web requests to back-end web applications.

The web tier in turn uses an internal NLB as the target for database traffic in another VPC. This works because of VPC peering, as no NLB works without basic network connectivity to the backend pool. Cross-zone load balancing is possible with NLB so that NLB interfaces in one AZ can use back-end pools that span AZs as a target.

This can be done for redundancy and if workloads are split unevenly between Availability Zones.

# Application Load Balancer

This load balancer is not likely to be one you manage as a network engineer, but you need to be aware of how it works from a network perspective. The difference between an ALB and an NLB is that an ALB uses application-level data to make load balancing decisions. It can use certain headers in a web request or the domain name in the SSL certificate., for example, to decide which web server back-end pool to forward requests.

Let's use what we know about NLB to understand how ALB works differently:

• ALB is allocated an IP and DNS name by AWS and these cannot be statically configured.

• ALB only listens on HTTP/HTTPS, NLB listens on just about anything.

• ALB terminates TLS/SSL connections and must have a certificate if using HTTPS. NLBs CAN do this but can also simply pass through connections to back-end servers to terminate the tunnel.

• ALB inspects application layer data and is therefore much slower to process requests than an NLB.

• ALB creates the back-end connection to the target group instead of passing it through, meaning the source IP the server will see will be the ALB IP, not the original source. The original IP can be provided to servers via other means (X-Forward Header).

• ALBs health check can use application-layer health checking. Instead of simply checking if a server is listening on port 443, an ALB can check for specific web page content or server responses to determine if the server is working and ready to receive traffic.

• ALB Listener rules can be much more complex and based on application layer data.

• ALBs will not work with PrivateLink technology by default.

In addition to that list, ALBs support Security Groups to restrict what resources can communicate with it, and over which methods. This differs from an NLB that does not use SGs. The ALB can use some of the out-of-scope AWS services around distributed location-based routing like AWS Global Accelerator. Also specific to ALBs is the ability to route incoming connections to an AWS Lambda function, the serverless code execution space. The reasons why you might do this vary and, frankly, are beyond our scope.

Let's look at a common ALB deployment:

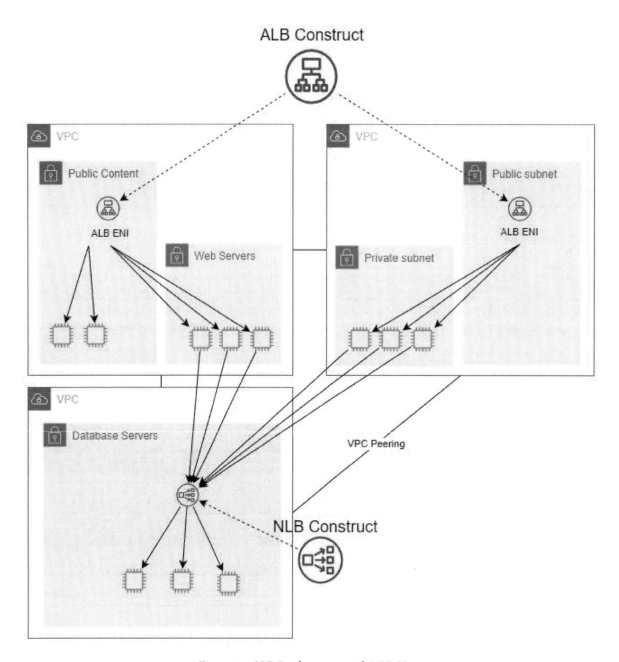

**Figure 54: ALB Deployment with NLB Tier**

You'll notice that the deployment is very much like how we deploy NLBs. The ALB creates an ENI in the subnets and requests to the ALB are sent to the ALB ENIs for creating connections to the target groups. Importantly, the ALB terminates the connection and sets up its own, it does not simply pass along the request.

There's a lot to ALBs, but honestly, the network part of them is very close to how NLBs work. The list above goes into the network differences to be aware of, but how an ALB works, how listeners and routing rules are configured, are well into the app-layer space and should not fall on the network engineers to own. If the ALB seems underwhelming, it's because it is like an iceberg. At the network layer we see only 20% of what an ALB is capable of, and we mostly just care that network connectivity to target groups exists and the SGs are correctly configured.

# Gateway Load Balancer

It seems fitting to finish off the main topics of this book with something like Gateway Load Balancer. It is a complex network construct that requires an understanding of the pieces of AWS networking that brought us to this point. This was briefly mentioned in the section on AWS Firewall, but the purpose of a GWLB is to make it much easier to insert some 3rd-party security appliances into a traffic flow in a scalable way.

Let's revisit a basic design using security NVAs from earlier to see how we can configure workload security:

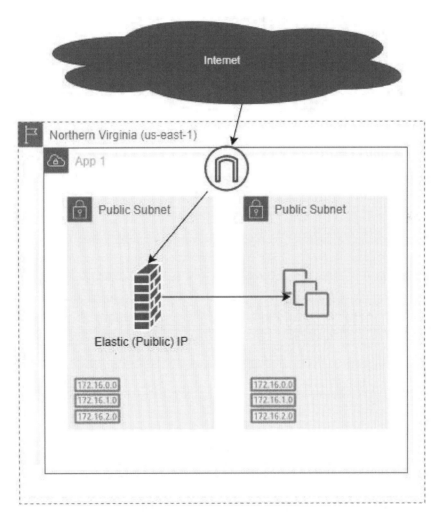

**Figure 27: IGW Ingress Use Case**

This is a perfectly working setup in which a firewall is inserted between a workload and the Internet for inspection. But it doesn't scale at all. Does every VPC need a firewall NVA to protect it?

What about TGW with a complex inspection VPC? It works, but it doesn't scale out very well because there is nothing governing what firewalls are being used for traffic flows. See below:

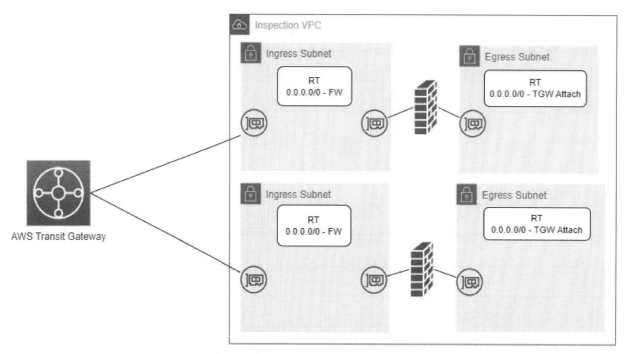

**Figure 21: Sample Inspection VPC/TGW Architecture**

This deployment has zone redundancy but does nothing to scale out. If more firewalls are needed, it will not be easy to add them in this setup because there is no load balancing for the different firewalls that may need to be added.

What is needed is an easy way to scale out security services without requiring that everything be manually routed to firewall instances as we scale outward and add more firewalls. This is where the GWLB comes in. We've already seen it once before in the context of AWS Firewall. As a refresher:

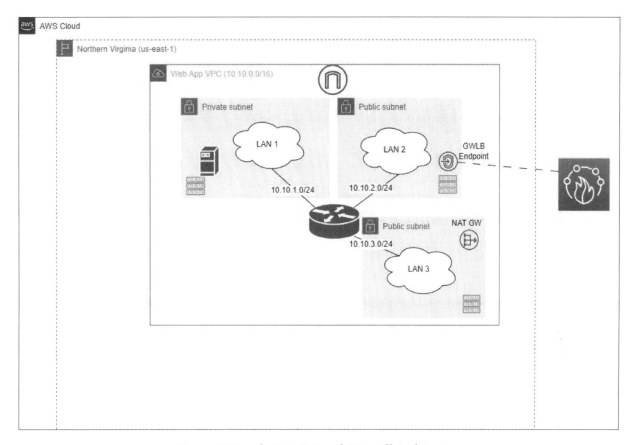

**Figure 47: Sample AWS Network Firewall Architecture**

Remember that in the case of AWS Firewall, GWLB endpoint is placed into the VPC as a route target, and the traffic to be inspected tunnels to a fleet of AWS firewall instances for inspection and (if allowed) returns with its source and destination unmodified.

GWLB allows us to do this with our own 3rd-party appliances, not just AWS services. The GWLB is a load balancer with a specific use case: to accept traffic, tunnel it under the AWS fabric to a 3rd party security appliance, and have it returned without affecting the packet from a routing perspective.

It accomplishes this feat using a tunnel protocol called GENEVE. The GWLB Endpoint is a tracked host object in the AWS fabric, as are most AWS endpoint services. The GWLB itself forms a GENEVE tunnel (similar to GRE, encapsulating traffic to deliver it while preserving the original source/destination) with the 3rd-party device. When the security appliance receives the packet from the GENEVE tunnel, it inspects the packet, and (if allowed) returns it to the GWLB over that GENEVE tunnel. The traffic is then returned to the GWLB endpoint in the VPC it came from, and routing continues normally.

This is reminiscent of most types of tunnel protocols. AWS creates the GWLB Endpoint (GWLBe) as a fabric construct to allow the AWS fabric to deliver traffic to the GWLB without having to worry about things like VPC peering or routing, and the GWLB does what all load balancers do: Checks the health of back-end resources and then forwards traffic to the back end for processing. In this case, the back end is another VPC entirely with 3rd-party appliances that can terminate GENEVE tunnels. The GWLB is managing things like session state and flow tracking, to ensure flows hit the same security appliance, this ensures the appliances see the full application flow for inspection.

Here's a diagram of what this looks like deployed:

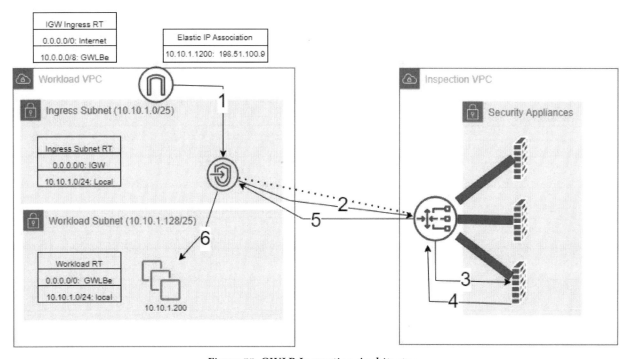

Figure 55: GWLB Inspection Architecture

Here's what happens:

1. A packet comes from the Internet destined to the public IP of this workload, 198.51.100.9. The IGW will perform the NAT to the local IP of the workload, 10.10.1.200. Consulting the IGW Ingress Route Table (Edge Association), it will forward the packet to the GWLBe in the Ingress subnet.

2. The GWLBe will use AWS PrivateLink technology to send the packet to the GWLB, where the GWLB will make a decision based on a hashing of 5-tuple (source/dest IP, source/dest port, protocol) information in the flow over which GENEVE tunnel to send the packet. It will keep this information sticky so the entire flow can hit the same appliance.

3. Remember in the Inspection VPC that the GENEVE tunnel is needed to preserve the original flow information and also so that the packet can be routed to the appliance. The Inspection VPC has no route to 10.10.1.200, so if GENEVE were not used the packet would be discarded as unrouteable. In this case the packet is delivered to the security appliance and inspected.

4. After inspection, assuming the flow is allowed, the packet is sent back to the GWLB over the GENEVE tunnel.

5. The GWLB removes the packet from the GENEVE tunnel and sends it back through PrivateLink to the original VPC.

6. The Ingress subnet RT is consulted as the packet enters the subnet and the next hop is local, so the packet is delivered to the workload. When the workload replies, the same flow happens in reverse because the Workload subnet RT uses the GWLB endpoint as the next hop for Internet-bound traffic, and after inspection, the Ingress VPC RT points to the IGW, and back to the Internet. And that's about it. There is more, of course, but from a network perspective, this should give plenty of understanding on how to discuss security inspection options with cloud teams.

# AWS Networking Lightning Round

We simply cannot cover everything in this book and have the book remain consumable to network engineers who are not trying to be cloud experts, who are short on time, and who just need to know enough cloud to build hybrid networks with cloud teams. The mission statement from the beginning has been to focus on the fundamentals as related to what network engineering we use every day, and to provide a quicker reference model to the entire cloud networking experience than 100 hours of AWS Training. This book is at best a bridge between traditional and cloud networking with a focus toward hybrid. Hybrid networking is where the dust will ultimately settle. Businesses will run things in the cloud that can benefit from elasticity and agility, and run the static, intensive workloads in a data center.

Not to miss the mark, this section is devoted to a high-level rollup of several AWS services that we don't have the space for or that don't need a detailed explanation. Each is important in its own space and the recommendation is to go further if needed. Each section will have links to further explore.

## AWS CloudWAN

AWS CloudWAN is an orchestration engine for connecting multiple transports together across the AWS backbone. The idea is you can bring an SD-WAN, a Direct Connect, a VPN,Transit Gateway, any connectivity that can connect to the cloud, and have CloudWAN orchestrate the connectivity between them and your current AWS VPC networks. You create a 'core' AWS CloudWAN network which builds a transit architecture policy, and then designate how you want to connect other sites to it. It is a hub and spoke architecture, the main benefit is using AWS to interconnect and using the CloudWAN interface to orchestrate the connectivity into one network. It supports hybrid networking but might end up being yet another GUI to manage depending on your current transit architecture.

Learn more: https://docs.aws.amazon.com/network-manager/latest/cloudwan/what-is-cloudwan.html

## AWS Outposts

AWS Outposts is a fancy term for, 'AWS Racks in your on-prem location'. The Outpost is connected to the AWS cloud via a link directly to the AWS backbone and comes with a rack full of compute, storage, and network equipment. AWS Outposts belong to an AWS region and can be managed as if it were just another AWS Availability Zone and subnet,but with far fewer options. You can deploy cloud resources to your outpost in a limited capacity and back up the storage locally, to S3, or another data storage option. The Outpost also includes a local gateway to connect to an on-prem network.

You pay for the rack and the usage, as with all things in the cloud. Outposts gives organizations the ability to extend the cloud down to an on-prem location.

Learn more: https://docs.aws.amazon.com/outposts/latest/userguide/what-is-outposts.html

# AWS Local Zone

The AWS Local Zone is slightly similar to Outposts, but it is basically an AWS-managed mini-AZ. Some cities and locations need faster connectivity to the AWS backbone, and so AWS has invested in small footprint DCs located near major areas in need of closer points of presence. These smaller DCs offer stripped-down AWS services,but faster connectivity to the AWS backbone if you fall within that geographic area.

As an example, if your business workloads are in the AWS Ohio region, but your data center is in New York City, there may be an AWS Local Zone in NYC to facilitate closer geographic connectivity to the Ohio region. Special care must be paid to Local Zones as there is usually no standard for what services (including virtual machine types) are available in a Local Zone.

Learn more: https://aws.amazon.com/about-aws/global-infrastructure/localzones/

# Kubernetes/Container Networking

We are really swinging for the fences trying to include a primer on K8/container networking in a lightning round, but let's see if we can hit it at a high level and show how container networking works inside the cluster as well as how traffic enters and leaves.

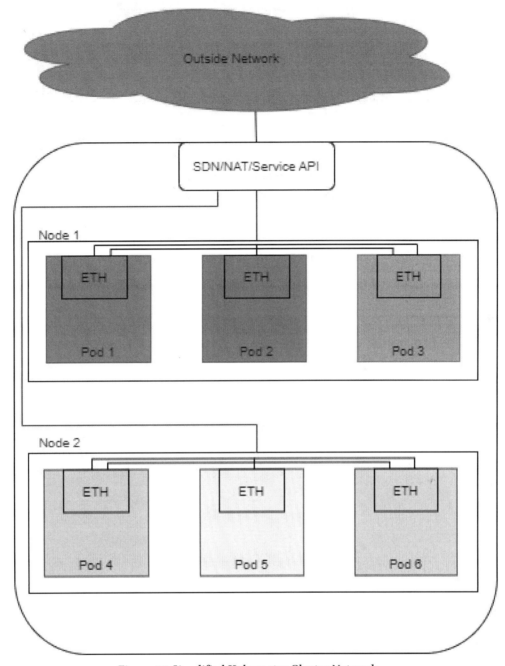

**Figure 56: Simplified Kubernetes Cluster Network**

This cluster is basically a large virtual machine running Linux. Inside the machine is a structured swarm of containers, each performing some function integral to the application that is running. The containers are ephemeral and often live only as long as the work they are processing. These containers often must communicate with other containers and resources outside the cluster. This requires that the controller that manages the cluster assign IP addresses to these containers. Commonly, the network within the clusters themselves can use non-routable space such as CG-NAT (100.64.0.0/10), good only within the cluster itself. As containers are created and destroyed the controller tracks the IP address allocations so that containers can communicate with each other.

If traffic is to leave the cluster, then each controller manages a Service API or some form of software-controlled NAT service that handles traffic leaving and entering the cluster in the same way we would expect a traditional NAT device to. Usually each cluster has a single 'external' IP for communication between all cluster containers and the outside. This IP just needs to be routable in the outside network.

If you think about it, it's very much like a classic firewall with a single public IP and a PAT set up for users behind it. Each user can reach the Internet and the firewall is multiplexing the connections with PAT, utilizing a single public IP. Traffic incoming to the container from the outside is a bit more complex and usually involves the Service API of the container expecting the incoming traffic to match some pattern so it can farm the connection to a backend container of relevance, just like the load balancers we discussed prior to this section.

# A Sincere Thanks

It is very much hoped that this book filled a gap that existed in your knowledge and did so in a way that was relevant to you. It is infinitely more difficult to swim at a depth between beginner and expert than at either extreme. I hope this book came close to its target and the intended goals of educating network engineers on cloud networking without requiring they become experts.

From here, the options are to continue this journey and learn more, focusing on what is relevant to the work you do, or try to keep the cloud at arm's length. The next sections are meant to help in any case. I sincerely hope that this has been a useful book to you and that I am able to write more in the future. Thank you for supporting me in whatever capacity you have, and I look forward to continuing to grow and give back to the tech industry.

# Acknowledgements

I also feel compelled to list the people who helped make this book a reality, whether it be via reviewing the material or help with navigating the publishing world.

Sincere thanks to:

Du'An Lightfoot

Stuart Clark

Eric Chou

Steve DiCicco

Riikka Sihvonen

Brian Pavane

Alex Perkins

Chris Miles

Jonathan Tetterton

Hiroko Nishimura

And the Secret Ninja Pirates, specifically,

Joel Sprague

Antony Sytnik

David Gaytan

# About The Author

Tim McConnaughy has been working in the tech industry for over 15 years. He has been a network engineer for most of that time, starting in a NOC, moving to engineering, and then spent time at Cisco as a network architect. He has a CCIE in Routing/Switching / Enterprise Infrastructure, #58615, and also has the AWS Solutions Architect Associate and Advanced Networking Specialty certificatons. He is also a cloud networking Solutions Architect at Aviatrix.

He lives in Raleigh, North Carolina, has a wife, two daughters, two cats, and a dog.

# Appendix: Links and Resources

## VPC

https://docs.aws.amazon.com/vpc/latest/userguide/configure-your-vpc.html

## Route Table

https://docs.aws.amazon.com/vpc/latest/userguide/VPC_Route_Tables.html

## Subnets

https://docs.aws.amazon.com/vpc/latest/userguide/working-with-subnets.html

## VPC Peering

https://docs.aws.amazon.com/vpc/latest/peering/what-is-vpc-peering.html

## NAT Gateway

https://docs.aws.amazon.com/vpc/latest/userguide/vpc-nat-gateway.html

## AWS VPN Options

https://docs.aws.amazon.com/vpc/latest/userguide/vpn-connections.html

## Site to Site VPN

https://docs.aws.amazon.com/vpn/latest/s2svpn/VPC_VPN.html

## Traffic Mirroring Guide (NOT COVERED)

https://docs.aws.amazon.com/vpc/latest/mirroring/what-is-traffic-mirroring.html

## AWS VPC IP Manager (NOT COVERED)

https://docs.aws.amazon.com/vpc/latest/ipam/what-it-is-ipam.html

## Transit Gateway

https://docs.aws.amazon.com/vpc/latest/tgw/what-is-transit-gateway.html

## Direct Connect

https://docs.aws.amazon.com/directconnect/latest/UserGuide/Welcome.html

## AWS Client VPN

https://docs.aws.amazon.com/vpn/latest/clientvpn-admin/what-is.html

## Security Groups

https://docs.aws.amazon.com/vpc/latest/userguide/VPC_SecurityGroups.html

## AWS Network Firewall

https://docs.aws.amazon.com/network-firewall/latest/developerguide/what-is-aws-network-firewall.html

## Local Zones and Outposts

https://docs.aws.amazon.com/vpc/latest/userguide/Extend_VPCs.html

## Toni Pasanen's Book: AWS Networking Fundamentals

https://leanpub.com/aws-networking-fundamentals

# Cloud Networking Quick Reference

On a phone call and scrambling to remember what these acronyms mean? Sure, you read the book, but it's a lot to memorize! Here's a handy quick reference guide for the times you are on a call with the cloud team and need to speak the language – fast. Hopefully this is a refresher instead of the first thing you read, but you bought the book, use it however you want!

| AWS Term | Short Description | Reference |
|---|---|---|
| Application Load Balancer (ALB) | One of several AWS Elastic Load Balancers. L7 load balancing only. Can act on HTTP/HTTPs only, using app-layer data for load balancing decisions and for health checking on app servers. MUST terminate SSL/TLS, cannot pass through encrypted traffic. | Chapter 6 |
| AWS Client VPN | Client VPN using OpenVPN. Very basic authentication/feature with SAML/IDP integration or using AWS Active Directory. Can attach to a VPC to give access to resources or be routed to other resources | Chapter 4 |
| AWS Network Firewall | AWS managed service that combines Route Tables, Endpoints with Gateway Load Balancer and AWS Firewall Manager GUI to provide inspection services in a VPC or attached to TGW. Provides L3-L7 security with IDS/IPS but management of rules can be complex and kludgy with web interface. | Chapter 5 |

| Elastic Network Interface (ENI) | SDN Host Tracking object. Similar to VM NIC. Can be attached and detached from other objects such as VMs and some AWS network services. ENI is tied to subnet and must use an IP from the subnet. If attached to an NVA/VM it will show as a network interface in the OS | Chapter 1 |
|---|---|---|
| Elastic IP (EIP) | SDN construct that reserves a public IP address from the AWS pool of public IPs. The EIP can be associated to an ENI and when the ENI is used within a subnet in a VPC, the IGW attached to the VPC will create a 1:1 NAT for the EIP mapping to perform static NAT to the Internet or AWS public services | Chapter 3, Chapter 6 |
| Endpoint | AWS SDN host tracking object. Can be added to a VPC to connect to a 3rd-party or AWS-owned service using PrivateLink. Requires the service to be known by catalog or invitation. | Chapter 2 |
| Gateway Load Balancer (GWLB) | One of several AWS Elastic Load Balancers. Special use case for 3rd-party security appliances. GWLB places an Endpoint into a VPC, traffic is routed to the endpoint and traffic is load balanced to 3rd-party appliances. GENEVE tunnel used between GWLB and appliance to preserve original source and destination and facilitate routing. Use for closest thing to 'bump in the wire' service insertion. | Chapter 6 |
| Internet Gateway (IGW) | SDN construct that serves as target for Route Table and which sets up Elastic IP associations for public IP addresses. Provides Internet connectivity for a single VPC but no PAT service. IGW can have custom Route Table with Edge Association | Chapter 3, Chapter 5, Chapter 6 |
| NAT Gateway (NAT GW) | AWS-managed NAT instance. Commonly used to PAT private hosts for Internet connection. Requires its own EIP. Traffic from private subnet is routed to NAT Gateway in public subnet, then NAT GW routes to IGW. Can also perform private NAT for two overlapping networks but each NAT GW only works in one direction. | Chapter 3 |
| Network Access Control List (NACL) | Exactly what it seems. Uses IPv4 and/or IPv6, Layer 4 information. Lower numbers are higher on the list. Can be applied to subnets in a VPC to restrict traffic. **STATELESS** and requires rules in both directions. ONLY useful when traffic enters or leaves a subnet. Use SG for intra-subnet traffic. | Chapter 5 |
| Network Load Balancer (NLB) | One of several AWS Elastic Load Balancers. L4 load balancing only. Can act on Layer 4 ports/protocols for load balancing decisions and health checking on app servers. CAN terminate SSL/TLS but can also forward encrypted traffic to back end server pools. MUCH faster than ALB. | Chapter 6 |
| Network Virtual | 3rd party virtual machines that perform a network function. Usually a vendor supported VM image utilizing the software and OS from that vendor. Examples include cloud routers and cloud firewalls. | Chapter 1, Chapter 2, Chapter 3, Chapter 4, Chapter 5 |

| | | |
|---|---|---|
| Appliance (NVA) | | |
| PrivateLink | AWS private attachment technology that creates connectivity between private resources using AWS underlay. See Endpoint | Chapter 2 |
| Route Table | Default or customized routing table. Can be applied to VPC, to individual subnets, to TGW attachments, and IGW as Edge Association. Similar to VRF. | Chapter 1 |
| Security Groups (SG) | VM/NIC level ACL. Can be applied closest to the ENI or service to restrict incoming and outgoing traffic. **STATEFUL.** Often used as microsegmentation. Limited rule set allowed. | Chapter 5 |
| Subnet | Carved from VPC supernet. Tied to Availability Zone. VM Resources and ENIs are deployed to subnets | Chapter 1 |
| Transit Gateway (TGW) | AWS-Managed routing instance. Allows static or dynamic (BGP) routing and supports multiple Route Tables for segmentation. Attaches to VPCs via ENI, can also be attached to Transit VIF and S2SVPN | Chapter 2, Chapter 4, Chapter 5 |
| Virtual Interface (VIF) | Connection to AWS cloud resources via DX. VIF can be classified as public (to Public services in any region), private (to customer resources in one region) or Transit (connection to a TGW in one region). Physically a VLAN allocated on a DX | Chapter 4 |
| Virtual Private Gateway (VGW) | AWS SDN object representing a fabric endpoint. The VGW can be attached to a VPC and does not reside within a subnet. Used to terminate outside connections to a VPC whether it be Site to Site VPN (with CGW) or Direct Connect. Can be set to propagate learned routes or advertise routes statically | Chapter 4 |
| VPC | Single route domain, basic network construct into which most resources are built. Created with primary supernet, minimum /29, maximum /16 | Chapter 1 |
| VPC Peering | Native cloud connection between two VPCs. Uses AWS underlay. VPC peer becomes object for Route Table destination to send traffic between VPCs. Not transitive, VPC A > B > C will not let VPC A > C | Chapter 2 |
| VPC Router | SDN construct that manages delivery of packets within a VPC using the Route Table. Does not exist, is not in data plane | Chapter 1 |

Printed in Poland
by Amazon Fulfillment
Poland Sp. z o.o., Wrocław

20892247R10078